The Law of Creation

THE SCIENCE BEHIND MANIFESTING YOUR DESIRES

It is your inherent right to live a life of limitless joy, happiness, health and wealth

By
Steve and Tracy Webster

This book is in your hands for a reason. You found it, and it found you. Somewhere in your subconscious mind you attracted it to help you change what you currently perceive as a life not filled with limitless abundance.

As you read this, there will be things that you resonate with and some that you don't. Given time, you may also learn to resonate with other aspects of this book.

May we recommend, as you read, that you make generous use of a highlighter.

When the soul is ready, the Universe responds!

The Law of Creation

©2020 Steve and Tracy Webster

ISBN: 978-0-578-66101-8

Table of Contents

Chapter 1 – Genesis, or How It all Began... by Steve

Growing up, we never had much money. Looking back, I guess we were middle class, but the 'middle class' always seemed to have money to spend, and I certainly did not. My friends had the latest toys, cool bikes and if there was something they really wanted, they seemed to get it.

Fast forward to University, and I still had no money. Around me students were freely spending on accessories, food, going out at night, and they all had cars. My girlfriend at the time left me, because I could never afford to take her anywhere. I was pretty miserable, so I left my studies and got a job.

I got a job as a computer operator, the lowest of the low in the information technology world, and of course it did not pay much. My job involved tedious night shift work and was not very challenging for an intelligent person. I bought a car so I could get to work, I lived with my parents, so I did not have to pay rent, and I was still broke part way through the month. I was generally a happy person, but the money situation was always quite depressing.

Fast forward 20 years, and things were very different. I lived in a beautiful 18,500 square foot home in an upmarket suburb, had (still do!) a beautiful wife, owned several luxury cars, 3 holiday homes dotted around the country, and a 3000-acre game farm (safari). I had all the latest toys including two light aircraft, jet skis, and quads. I was the CEO and founder of 3 successful companies, which earned about $100M+ per year and employed 250 people. I obtained an MBA, thus removing the 'guilt' of having left University so many years before.

So how did I get from zero to hero? Well, I had uncovered a method that attracted this wealth. I did not know it at the time, but I was using fundamental tools such as gratitude that are the building blocks of the Law of Creation. Only some time later in life did I sit down and assess what I was doing and wrote it down - which then became the framework for this book.

Being mindful and using your conscious and subconscious mind to create wealth takes time and effort, and over time I would become lazy and stop practicing what I knew. Slowly the wealth would dwindle, and after a while I would have to remind myself to re-employ my knowledge of what had previously worked and brought wealth and success. Sure enough, the wealth would increase again. So, I know it works, because every time I decide to use it, I see tangible evidence.

In 2006, The Secret was released. It was interesting, but I knew deep down that it only portrayed a piece of what was required to Create your life. It suggested that the path to success involves practicing visualization and gratitude, but it did not explain how visualization and gratitude affected the scientific Universe to bring wealth and success. This book explains why concepts like The Secret work, and also why it DOES NOT work. In essence, there are 18 Laws of Creation but The Secret and many Law of Attraction programs only cover two of them. It is not vital that you know and understand all of these Laws; but it helps your Creation ability when you understand how the Laws affect your life, and the outcome of what you have Created.

I have used the techniques in this book to regularly attract wealth, lose it and attract it again, almost at will. I have used these techniques over time to create a company earning $100M a year, write and publish books, become a pilot, develop a board game, an app for the board game, and produce a movie, amongst other things. I have a deep-seated understanding of what works to bring success, and - even better - in this book I will explain WHY it works.

Some of the explanations involve scientific and physics principles such as quantum theory and wave function. As far as I know this is the first time we have ever seen the Laws of Creation defined in practical terms, and not just theory. Some people do not need to know how it works; they just need to know that it does. Like switching your car on and driving it. If you are that kind of person, you can skip the science! However, if you are a left brained person who is generally critical or skeptical about the slew of woo-woo theories that pervade the market then the scientific process is explained herein.

This book will explain why concepts such as prayer are effective. The people who believe in prayer know that it works, but they do not know the why or how. The general feeling is that 'God' listened and delivered the goods. Here is a shocking fact: YOU are that GOD*. The power is within you. YOU create your world, your life, your Universe. At some stage you have given away your power to create. It is time to take it back and start Creating.

Certain 'ingredients' are required for you to start changing your life, for you to become a Master Creator:

- ❖ Higher consciousness (allows you to have more resources, to learn pause, to vibrate at a higher level and to understand the power of the human heart and the subconscious mind)
- ❖ Understanding of the electromagnetic nature of the Universe
- ❖ Understanding of the 18 Laws of Creation (how they work individually and synergistically)
- ❖ Learning to embrace positivity and lessen negativity
- ❖ Understanding the immense physical power of gratitude
- ❖ Understanding the infinite nature of the Universe

This book is a 'Creator's Manual'. All these elements are discussed, detailed and explained, sometimes to a scientific level.

Read on and start Creating!

*Even if you are conservatively religious, the scriptures say that you were created in God's image. Ergo God made you and equipped you with God's powers, right?

> God is the giver and the gift; man is the receiver. God dwells in man, and this means that the treasure house of infinite riches is within you and all around you. By learning the laws of mind, you can extract from that infinite storehouse within you everything you need to live life gloriously, joyously and abundantly.
>
> Joseph Murphy

Chapter 2 – The Important Information

You Have the Ability to Create Anything You Desire

It is your innate right to live a life of limitless joy, happiness, health and wealth! Why then do most people not achieve this state?

As we go about our daily lives, we all seek out knowledge; we try to improve our lives, and obtain more joy, happiness and purpose. Inherent in that statement is that knowledge is the key to these things: joy, happiness and purpose. That knowledge resides within us, but we remain 'unconnected' to it. When we come across knowledge that we find interesting, or that we resonate with, we absorb that information. Yet what we are really doing is unlocking the information that is already stored within us. So, it is really more of a 'remembering'. You reconnect with that information – in effect you "re-member" yourself to that knowledge.

Nothing is more desirable than possessing the ability to create:

- ❖ to create our life
- ❖ to change our circumstances
- ❖ to manifest abundance
- ❖ to emit and absorb joy
- ❖ to develop harmonious bonds with family and friends
- ❖ to establish meaningful relationship with our significant others
- ❖ to emanate love
- ❖ to establish purpose

We all have this ability to create. It is innate within us, it is inherent in every one of us, it is part of who we are. We are just 'cut off' from it. We are disconnected from it. This book is all about how to reconnect to your creative powers.

You have created the life you are currently living. The fact is you might not be happy with it - the fact that you are reading this book suggests you want changes - and you may wish for things to be different. The key to fixing this is firstly understanding how we created what we have (so far), and secondly understanding why we are unable to manifest what we consciously desire.

You are perfect, and you are immensely powerful. You just need to reconnect with that power. This power is Universal, divine, infinite, boundless – and you have a divine right to it. This book will show you how to reconnect yourself to the amazing ability to create everything you want, and everything you desire.

You are the Creator of your life. In terms of relativity, you are at the center of your creation. When you realize this, ironically you become 'more centered'. When you think someone, something or somewhere else is the center of what's going on, you are giving your power away to the external world. Stop. Re-center. 'Re-realize' your role in this and become the Creator again. Each and every day acknowledge the conscious aspect that you are the center of your Universe. Over time you will see the World move to meet you, and you will not have to do the heavy lifting. Your life becomes more stable, more peaceful, and you assume a sense of purpose. Ultimately you will control the time and space around you.

Why the Law of Attraction Cannot Work on its Own

The Law of Attraction was recently popularized with the release of the Abraham books by Jerry and Esther Hicks, and of course *The Secret*.

The Law of Attraction is only one of the 18 Laws of Creation. Therefore, if you practice the Law of Attraction on its own, you are only applying one eighteenth of the Law of Creation. So, to some extent applying this law will work, and may bring manifestation. However, if one incorporates and applies all eighteen laws, you will be far more powerful in your creative abilities. If you only practice the Law of Attraction you are ignoring 17 other strong laws of creation, and you are attempting to create without the most powerful law – the Law of Gratitude.

In describing the Law of Attraction, popular books such as *The Secret* state that "Everything that exists, has a certain frequency (vibration), and that frequencies work magnetically. So, everything that you create, attracts more of the same." But this is not technically correct, because in magnetism "like repels like." Ergo if attracting wealth was a result of magnetism, once you had wealth you would then repel wealth. This is not what we want, nor is it how it works. There is however the Law of Gratitude, where you resonate with what you have, and so the Universe gives you more of it. And many other laws have an impact on what you are attracting into your life.

Rather than a magnet, think in terms of a radio set. Your "transmitter" sends out messages to the Universe. The Universe sends events and information back to you based on a similar frequency. Your "receiver" is set to the same frequency as your transmitter. The more powerful your receiver, the more powerful you are in creating and attracting. If your transmitter is set to 'low' frequencies – shame, guilt, judgement – then you will attract low frequency experiences. Conversely, if your transmitter is set to 'high' frequencies – joy, love, abundance – then you will attract high frequency experiences.

We only see the world from our level of understanding. I go into detail on this later in the book, where I explain that our low consciousness physically restricts our conscious understanding.

Many aspects of this book would have been considered 'woo-woo', ethereal or fantasy. However, with the recent discoveries in the quantum world, we are beginning to realize the power of individuals in the role of shaping our Universe. There is no doubt that our minds created this Universe. If that is true, and it is, then it is obvious that we can create whatever we put our minds to.

Chapter 3 – The Nuts and Bolts

Law of Creation Formula

The "simple" formula is indeed very simple:

Visualization + Enthused Emotion = Manifestation

But there are mechanics behind this "simple formula" which need to be understood, and mastered, in order to easily display your powers of creation. It is like driving a car: if you watch somebody driving the car it looks effortless and easy. But it took a while for the person to learn how to drive. In addition, they have an understanding of the mechanics of the car, safety protocols, rules of the road, etc. Without these elements they could not effortlessly drive the car.

It is the same with the Law of Creation; when you understand the elements involved, and put them into practice, your manifestation abilities become effortless. The more you understand, and the more practice you have in creating, the more effortless it becomes! When you understand all 18 laws, you will understand the relative strength and weakness of the Law of Attraction. You will also learn how the other laws 'amplify' the Law of Attraction.

The 18 Laws of Creation

1. **Law of Attraction** – The energy you send out to the Universe acts in a strange way. In effect, you attract the same energy that you are constantly emitting. The more constant you are in the energy and vibration level you are emitting, the more and better you will attract energies at the same vibration. At our basest level we are electromagnetic energy which is made up of light photons. This energy is within us, and whether we like it or not we emit this energy into the world around us. Being cognizant of this fact is the first step in understanding the law of attraction. Our conscious mind emits a weak form of energy, and our subconscious emits a far more powerful signal. Mastering the law of attraction entails understanding how and why the subconscious mind is more powerful

and is able to manifest so easily. The essence of this book is explaining how you re-program your subconscious to deliver to you the world that you desire.

2. **Law of Reverse Action** – This dictates that any idea, vision, or concept that resides in your <u>subconscious</u> will manifest, and will override any <u>conscious</u> idea, vision or concept. Any desire you have in a conscious form is relatively powerless. If we program it into our subconscious (and there are many ways to do this) only then does action take place. The 'reverse' part is that the more we try to make something happen with our conscious mind, the further we push it away. Conversely, the more we create with our subconscious, the more we manifest. This is also known as **The Law of Reverse Effort** – With your conscious mind you try very hard to change your thinking, your life, and your circumstances, often with little or no result (weight loss, anybody?). This is most people's experience with the "common" understanding of the Law of Attraction. Your subconscious mind is very powerful; when you let your subconscious mind do the heavy lifting, results start to happen. A good example is outlined later in the section on gratitude: a real-life story of a billionaire who practiced a fifteen-minute gratitude session every day which attracted his wealth— would you rather physically work eight hours a day, or spend fifteen minutes a day creating wealth?

3. **The Law of Repetition** – The more we do something, the better we become at it, and the more acceptable it is to us. By repeating your idea, or more accurately: by repeatedly visualizing with enthused emotion your idea, vision or concept as often as you can, it starts to take root. Like all the laws there is a scientific and logical explanation for this. In our brain we have neural pathways, these are the electrical circuits our brain follows when accessing information or executing any behavior. When we start a new memory or behavior the brain establishes a tentative and weak pathway. But the brain is efficient and prefers well-worn and established neurological pathways – the brain uses most of your body's energy and it uses less energy this way. This is why it is so difficult to change an established habit or behavior. The more we use a particular pathway, the more

established it becomes. After twenty-one days of constant use of this new pathway, the pathway becomes a highway in your brain and any behavior automatically becomes a habit. In essence, it is the concept of 'attention' amplifies 'intention'. Keep repeating, with visualization and enthused emotion your idea, vision and concept!

4. **Law of Probability** – Focus produces results. The more we concentrate on a specific outcome, the more likely that outcome will manifest. Again, this has a scientific basis and in Chapter 5 I prove physically how concentrating on a specific outcome has a greater probability of manifesting that outcome. Another positive aspect of this law is the fact that the more you concentrate on something, the more inclined your subconscious is to believe it, and achieve it. Know that your power works, and it gets stronger with use, like exercising a muscle.

5. **The Law of Dominance** – The more you believe in your idea, vision or concept, the more real you make it. This is verified by the religious "faith can move mountains" beliefs, and the "if you think you can, you are right" statement. The more dominant a belief is in your head, the more likely it is that the belief will manifest. There is a dynamic circular action between all the laws: a thought repeated often enough, and with strong feeling will become entrenched in the subconscious, and ultimately will manifest. Continued manifestations then lend belief and credibility to your ability to create, thus empowering the act of you creating. The reason you have adopted your parents' faith, values and beliefs is that you have been exposed to them over a period of time. In turn, they have programmed you to accept them because they were regularly shared with you, so often that you now accept them as your beliefs. Ergo, keep telling yourself positive affirmations and keep visualizing the preferred outcome; it is only a matter of time before your Mind accepts these things as immutable facts.

6. **The Law of Delayed Action** – Some people get disheartened because they do not see instant or rapid materialization of their idea, vision or concept. Trust that the Universe has a Grand Plan, and that things

will happen when they are supposed to. This incorporates letting go, and not being attached to the result. But that is incongruous – if we are not attached to the result why do we want that result? By all means be attached to the result, but only with your subconscious mind! With our conscious mind we "tell" the Universe what we want, how we want it, and send a simultaneous message about how desperate we are to have it. This is a "push" process, where we try and force our perception onto the Universe. Conversely with our subconscious mind, once we have it programmed correctly, it "tells" the Universe how we will *feel* when a specific manifestation has occurred.   It focuses on the end result. This is a "pull" process. The conscious mind tries to use force, the subconscious mind uses power. Thoughts take time to flow, to ripple through the Universe. Thoughts do not manifest immediately. Who and what you are now, is not an instant creation. It is a creation made up of the flow of yesteryear's thoughts and emotions, this lifetime's thoughts and emotions, and the thoughts and emotions from previous lifetimes and planes.

7. **The Law of Association** – Our perception of the world is affected by "good" and "bad" things that have happened to us through our lifetime. This programming is contained in our subconscious mind. If we grew up poor, and our parents always told us how hard life is, and how short money is, then that is our programming. If we think we are unhealthy then that is our programming, and we will tend to attract an unhealthy state. If we believe we are not good enough, then we remain in a state of unworthiness. So, if our association with money is lack and scarcity, then that is what we will experience. The solution is to change the associations we have with money, health, relationships, occupation, self-esteem and ability. Again, we do this by programming our subconscious mind. What you think subconsciously is what you become. As you continually think a specific thought, this becomes entrenched in the mind. You conjure up images related to the thought, and specific outcomes. As you continue to do this you are programming your subconscious mind. You are burning the outcome into your core self. Because of this, and based on all these laws, that is what you will manifest. The law of association affects our ability to create in another way: if you are

"good" at manifesting you will have a positive association with the act of creating, which leads to an upward spiral of positive creation: I can, I have the ability, and I will. Conversely if you had "bad" experiences when you attempted to manifest, then you will be naturally pessimistic about it. This leads to a downward spiral: I tried before and it did not work, ergo I do not have the ability, and it does not work.

8. **Law of Auxiliary Emotion (Law of Intensity)** – The intensity of a thought, suggestion or mental image is proportional to the emotion that accompanies it. If the suggestion invoked a weak emotion, it sits but is not firmly anchored in the subconscious. If the suggestion evoked a strong emotion, it is firmly rooted in the subconscious. This is why you need a burst of feel-good energy to "energize" the idea, vision, or concept and "burn" it into your subconscious. When you imagine what you are trying to manifest, focus on the feeling you will have and experience when that thing has manifested. The more intensely you can visualize, imagine or feel the emotion, the stronger the programming into your subconscious. An example of this is PTS (this used to be termed PTSD) is very difficult to treat. The main reason is the associated terror at the time of the traumatic event. Terror is an intense emotion, which causes a large release of memory chemicals (hormones and neurotransmitters) to be secreted. The PTS event thus becomes deeply rooted in the subconscious, sadly with the associated negative aspects. In terms of electromagnetic energy, the heart is a more powerful transmitter than the brain; therefore, what we *feel* is more powerful than what we consciously *think*.

9. **Law of Pessimistic Interpretation** – If a statement can be interpreted either optimistically or pessimistically, some people will interpret it as pessimistic. Dr. Dabney Ewin explains that this is protection against perceived danger: "An antelope that sees the bushes moving and (pessimistically) moves away for fear it is a lion is more likely to survive than one that assumes it is a warthog and continues grazing." Put another way, when we have an expectation, we invoke the risk of the expectation not being met and increase the likelihood of being let down or rejection occurring. A pessimistic person does not

increase this risk, and in fact receives a perceived reward when they are "proven right" (when something goes wrong). When you have doubts about whether your idea, vision or concept will materialize or not, remember that humans are naturally pessimistic as a result of an inherent survival mechanism. An aspect of mastering your ability to create is to learn to override this pessimistic tendency. This pessimism comes from our lowest brain system, the amygdala, and is linked to primitive survival beliefs, and our reptilian brain. To overcome this, one needs to elevate to a higher consciousness, and override this lower level thought process. Focus on the Law of Association, where you think of times you have successfully manifested your desire. You can be driven by Love, or by Fear. It is your choice.

10. **Law of Perception (Law of Belief)** – If you believe something to be true, it is true for you. Regardless of the reality, you will behave accordingly when you consider something to be true. Keep telling yourself that your vision is true, and it will become so. The mind is a powerful creation tool, which you need to train and exercise. A thought with a known outcome is a fact. You realize what you desire. This is the law that makes any placebo 100% effective. The bible affirms this in Mark 11:24: "Therefore I tell you, whatever you ask in prayer, believe that you have received it, and it will be yours."

11. **The Law of Balance** – The nature of the Universe we live in is Balance. Don't forget that life is in balance, and there is a Grand Plan. For you to "receive" something, you must release something, or give something up, or not receive something that was intended for you. Be careful what you ask for, remain in integrity, and always be grateful for what you have. Remember that your Source knows what you need, and you muddy the waters by consciously asking for what you humanly desire. This is not negative in the human sense, but it may slow your spiritual journey, especially if what you desire is of material essence or fulfils our base desires (wealth, fancy car, nice house, attractive partner, etc.). Duality is a feature of this Earth plane, and we tend to judge things as 'good' or 'bad'. Hot and cold are not opposites, just different degrees on a single continuum, the same is

valid for good and bad. In reality everything is neutral, it is just how you perceive things that make it good or bad.

12. **The Law of Gratitude** – Being grateful ALWAYS attracts more of the same without you having to give something up—because you already have it. You are merely intensifying the quantity. Gratitude is an emotion that vibrates at such a high level that it has the power to attract experiences on a similar high vibrational level. Gratitude is the most powerful of the Laws of Creation. In Chapter 6: Increase your Potential, The Tools of the Trade, I cover Gratitude in more depth.

13. **The Law of Homeostasis** – Each of us has a program in our subconscious mind which is our "script" for how successful each of us will be. This is homeostasis, our mind's script which enforces our limitations, and sets the ceiling on our successes. But this script can be rewritten, and our subconscious minds can be "reprogrammed," using affirmations, gratitude, mindfulness (and other possible tools discussed later). If you do attract success above your homeostasis limit, ultimately you will not retain it. A quick example: think of the archetypal story of the person who wins a large amount of money on the Lottery; after a few years they have spent the money and typically have less than they started with. Their homeostasis dictated that they were poor, and that is what ultimately manifested. So, like exercising your body with weights, the homeostasis needs exercise to increase its set of values. The simple basis of homeostasis is "believe it—achieve it!", but at the level of the subconscious mind.

14. **Law of Resistance** – Resistance is fear. For as long as we resist something or somebody in our lives, we are showing fear. Fear is the opposite of attraction. In addition, resistance says that we are not happy with what we have created. Fear is a creational emotion, but sadly we create the event that we were fearing. This is a spiritual learning mechanism: spiritually there is nothing to fear, so we attract what we fear in order that we desensitize ourselves to the fear, thus ultimately eliminating it from our belief system. It has been scientifically proven that we bring about our fears. Psychologically our subconscious will bring about what we fear, so that we can face

it and move on without fear. Swimming upstream is laborious, it is far easier to 'go with the flow'. In a sense this means you being more accepting. You have limited resources – if you are spending these resources on resisting change, then you have less resources for creating.

15. **The Law of Diminishing Returns** – The harder you try with your conscious mind to design or create manifestations into your life, the less the subconscious will involve itself. A good example is where you force yourself to go to sleep at an earlier hour than normal as you have to wake up earlier, but sleep eludes you and you remain awake for a long time. If you let your subconscious mind do the heavy lifting, you will require minimal conscious will and effort to create. This is an important element of understanding your ability to create: when you create using your **conscious** mind, you create using your 'lower' mind which vibrates at a lower electromagnetic frequency – thus it is more difficult to create, and any creation is not as permanent. The world we live in is completely electromagnetic, and the subconscious mind is better equipped to create at this level. In a sense you are swimming against the flow – the natural flow of creative energy. When you create using your **subconscious mind**, you create using your 'higher' mind, which vibrates at a higher electromagnetic level – thus it seems easier to create, and any creation is more permanent.

16. **The Law of Cycles** – Things naturally go "well" for a while, and things then go "badly." Learn to appreciate the ups. Learn to accept the downs. Nothing is all good or all bad, so there is always something good in every situation. Find the good and acceptance will follow, especially if you also find gratitude for the good. Appreciation will increase the frequency and duration of the ups. A lesson will keep returning until you have learnt the lesson; acceptance of the downs will reduce their frequency and duration. What you focus on is what you attract. If you think of ten things in your life, probably eight are "good" and two are "bad". Why do you spend so much time and energy focusing on the two "bad" things? Remember that what you focus on is what you attract. Train yourself to rather focus on the eight "good" things, along with gratitude: you will automatically

attract more "good" things into your life. The Laws of Cycles, Balance and Gratitude are inextricably linked. This is the Triumvirate of Creation.

17. **The Law of Infinite Possibility** – This law may stretch the mind for some people. All outcomes currently exist: you as you are now, you as the opposite sex, you as an astronaut, etc. The reason that you are experiencing your current reality is because this is what your subconscious mind has manifested, based on all the inputs you have given it. This is the phenomenon that allows us to radically change our lives and manifest a life with joy, health, wealth and success. Chapter 5 goes into more detail on this (way more!) and physically proves this concept. Spiritual scientists refer to the third dimension which is what you see now - your current reality. The fourth dimension is what is possible, the ability to amend circumstances by pulling from the Field of Infinite Possibility. The physics of wave function allow this Field of Infinite Possibility.

18. **The Law of Vibration** - The Universe does not *hear* what you are asking for. It *feels* the vibration of what you are asking for. Because everything is energy, vibrating at a unique resonance, the Universe will offer matching outcomes based on this resonating vibrational frequency. You might think of yourself in human terms: small (relative to the Universe), flesh and blood, logical, emotional, chemically responsive. BUT the Universe does not respond to these things. It cannot. Remember everything is energy vibrating. This is the language of the Universe. If you want to converse with the Universe, you have to do it in the language the Universe understands – vibrational energy. As a human, the best tools you have for this are your heart and your subconscious mind.

The key to masterfully creating your new world is mastering the conscious mind. We must change our thoughts and values, and in essence change how we think. This is incredibly difficult, especially to begin with. If you have ever tried meditating, and gave up because it is difficult, or required too much concentration, then you know what I am talking about. For those of you who have tried meditating, and have mastered it, then learning the Laws of Creation will come much easier.

For those who struggle with it, don't give up. Ask your subconscious to allow it through when the time is right. But in terms of struggle, would you rather struggle 16 hours a day with your conscious life, or is it time for a change?

Chapter 4 – You the Creator

<u>We Create What We See</u>

I tell my kids all the time: "You have zero control over what happens around you. But you 100% control how you respond to it!" I'm not sure whether they truly 'get' this statement yet. But this is where your power lies. What we perceive as "reality" is a model of the world based upon our life, our experiences of events. We are all familiar enough with the Theory of Relativity to know that this model is seen from "your" viewpoint, based on your beliefs, your perspectives, and your physical limitations. In Neuro-Linguistic Programming terms "your map is not necessarily the territory". I'm sure you've seen the meme where there is a 6 or a 9 and dependent on your perspective you will perceive either the 6 or the 9 and both are right according to your individual perspective.

We base our model of the world heavily on our understanding of the data around us, and we **absolutely believe** that our version of the world is the only one. But, time after time, certain "pillars"—the foundations of our concrete beliefs—get shifted, change, or are removed. Have you ever been so certain of something only to have additional information surface that shifts what you think or believe? We then have to "re-calibrate" the model of our world. Time, technology and consciousness levels all lend themselves to converting our "reality" to a new level of truth, and that is not necessarily reality either—it may also change based on time, technology and consciousness.

The picture of our world constantly changes as we acquire more information. Our version of the information is generally not the same as another person's, which explains why we all see the world so differently. Your version of the world is not necessarily correct. And because everything is relative, it probably **is not** correct.

Sadly, not only do we tend to misperceive our reality, we skew that perception towards the negative things that happen to us. According to Rick Hanson (PhD): "Negative stimuli produce more neural activity than . . . positive stimuli. Negatives are also perceived more easily and quickly.

For example, people in studies can identify angry faces faster than happy ones. Negative events and experiences get quickly stored in memory—in contrast to positive events and experiences, which usually need to be held in awareness for a dozen or more seconds to transfer from short-term memory buffers to long-term storage."

There are two reasons why we focus more on the negative aspects of our life, and why these negative aspects are more intensely "burned" into our memory than the positive aspects; the first is self-preservation. In prehistoric times there were many dangers in the environment; if a danger presented itself, we needed to focus quickly and bring about all our fight or flight resources in an obvious response. So, our primitive brain is wired to be on the constant alert for negative (dangerous) signals, to amplify these to make us focus on them, and then respond to the danger. We naturally focus more on the negative as a survival tool.

The second reason is the Law of Intensity. In simple terms, the intensity of any memory is relative to the intensity of the emotion at the time of the event. If Mom bought us an ice cream when we were four years old, this is a good memory but has low intensity; chances are we cannot recall the event. If we had a serious car accident when we were fourteen, this is burned into our memory because it carries the intensity of the fear that was experienced. As mentioned earlier terror is an intense emotion and therefore PTS memories are deeply ingrained into a person's psyche.

Your memory is weak or strong depending on the emotion at the time of the event. The emotions affected the type and quantity of hormones and neurotransmitters into your brain. In the same way, when you feel the *emotion* of having something, your body releases these chemicals. I call it emoticising! The emotion you apply will have the effect of 'e-motion', energizing the motion of the thing you want to attract into your life. Another way of looking at it is that 'e-motion' is an abbreviation for electromagnetic motion.

So, we might have a semi-scientific explanation for why we focus on the negative more than the positive, and why the negative memories are stronger, but we still have some choice as to how we react to these messages. It is in the exercising of this choice that we move closer to, or further away from, a higher consciousness. If we opt to use our primitive brain responses, then we opt for fight or flight. If we opt to use our higher brain responses, then we suppress or repress the emotions and memories and we react from a more rational mindset. If we choose to use our higher brain responses, then we can choose to ignore, delete, modify, accept and forgive. Obviously, these latter choices are operated from a higher functioning individual, a person at a higher "consciousness" than their primitive or emotional brains. You have a 'choice' muscle - the ability to choose how we respond to something is an inalienable power – and this choice muscle takes time to develop. Like learning to meditate, 'choosing' how you react is an art that takes time and practice to perfect.

We must accept that the world we have created is our responsibility. In this way, we take back the power to create. When we blame others or circumstances then we project a sense of blame, guilt and shame. When we judge, we are in fact judging ourselves, because we have created the situation. Nothing in your life occurs without your participation. When you accept this fact, this is the first step to you reasserting your rightful place as Creator of your Universe. Let me stress that for as long as you blame others for your situation you are telling the Universe that you are a victim and not a Creator. Are you a victim or a Creator?

> **You are a self-observing system observing your own creation**
>
> **Confucius**

The Illusion of Reality

To each of us, what we see we perceive as real. For instance, the book you are currently holding in your hands, or the screen you are currently using to read these words. But amazingly, nothing in our world is 'solid'. All that you perceive is formed from a lattice which has energy at its source. This lattice is basically a temporary physical form around empty space. Everything in the Universe is essentially 99.99999999% empty space. Can you believe that if you removed all the 'space', the entire human race would fit into the size of a sugar cube.

I know it's hard to fathom, but nothing is 'solid' in our Universe. An object that appears solid is only a subtle entity formed by an invisible vibration. This form is shaped by the Observer – you. In this sense, each of us creates the World around us. These invisible vibrations manifest as geometrical figures and in this way create a crystal-like entity. The design of a snowflake, the shape of a flower, and everything you see takes on their form because they are responding to an invisible vibration. Stars, planets, minerals, plants, animals and human beings are invisible music that has taken on visible form. It is invisible to us because of our low 'consciousness' state – our spectrum of understanding is not wide enough to fathom the incredible infiniteness of everything.

The Illusion of Separation

A photon travels, it is what a photon does. The energy it contains propels it in constant motion. The momentum of its energy is the determining factor of its vibration level. The denser an object is, the slower it "moves" and the lower its vibration level. A photon vibrates higher than a human, which vibrates higher than a rock—even though we are all made up of the same "material."

As per Heisenberg's Uncertainty Principle, you can measure either a photon's speed OR its position—not both. You, the observer, have chosen to slow down photons so that they appear in a material form; you see your body, your house, your car, and the world around you. All of this is low vibrating because it is dense and has visible form—you have chosen to "fix" its position. Because you have now observed its position you cannot observe its momentum (vibration). In this regard you are "creating" what you see, you are creating your world and everything in it. It is your conscious mind, which vibrates at a low level, which chooses to observe and "fix" the photons, in effect creating everything around you. Your subconscious mind vibrates at a higher level, and does not "fix" the photons, allowing the energy to perform continuous movement. If you were to lose the ego, your conscious mind, you would dispel the illusion around you because you no longer choose to create it (it is your act of observing that creates). This is what A Course in Miracles refers to when it talks about the illusion of separation. This is what the Bible means when it refers to man separating himself from God. "Sin" is the Latin word meaning to go without; in this case you choose to observe and create the Earth and go without the pure spiritual energy that would be present if you did not observe it.

Faith healers use this concept to heal people; they choose to see a different outcome, and in their minds they "fix" the photons to show the client as healthy and whole—for instance a wound healing. It is their strong belief, and their intent, and the client's belief in the healer's ability, which leads to the healing. It is the reason why placebos work.

The basic rule of quantum physics is that something can only "come" into existence **when it is observed**. That means that something can only exist if somebody's mind **first thought it into existence**! Do you now see how you create your world?

The Law of Probability

In Chapter 5 I cover in detail the science behind The Law of Creation and explain things such as the "probability density function" and the Schrodinger equation. I refer to it here as it is pertinent in showing how you are the Creator of your own world. Physics proves that you are the Creator (at least, of your "little" world!); Physicist Max Born developed the "probability density function" in the Schrödinger equation. When a photon acts like a wave, and it meets an interference (e.g. slits in a wall) it creates peaks and troughs. Born stated that the peaks indicate likely areas of the photon being present, and the troughs indicate least likely areas for the photon being present; this makes sense, because statistically, over time, more photons in one area created the peak witnessed. Here's the shocker - YOU affect that likelihood. The energy you send out arranges a more probable, or less probable, arrangement of the photons. In effect, the energy you emit creates the likelihood of the outcome! You are a Probability Machine.

Energy forms the basis for photons, bio-photons, light waves, sound waves, gravity waves and magnetic waves. Everything is made up of photons, which are made from energy. You create your reality in two ways: firstly, by fixing the positions of the photons, and secondly through your electromagnetic energy vibration. Consider this: even a piece of food emits photons—this is what the nose detects when it "smells" food. You are constantly emitting photons, which are in vibration with your thoughts and emotions. You are a walking photon emitter.

Light, at its basest level, is information; the observer of the light determines its form, but this specific form is only for that specific observer. All electromagnetic waves have a property of frequency (how many waves per second) and amplitude (the energy of the wave). Time speeds up and slows down depending on the position of the observer (Einstein's relativity), which affects frequency. So even the frequencies of electromagnetic waves are different for every observer. What you see is different from what any other observer is seeing. We know that photons exist in all possible positions at once – this is called quantum superposition – and our act of observing causes the photons to take subtle form – this is called quantum wave function collapse.

Because reality is flashing in and out of existence (hypothetically at Planck time – 10^{44} times per second – as explained by The Resonance Project biophysicist William Brown), every time our reality oscillates between form, and the pure energy state of the field, our awareness which is constant and doesn't flash in and out of existence *informs the field what to reappear as* when it makes its transition back to form at the quantum level.

Therefore each time we oscillate into formlessness, we have complete and total control and *responsibility* over what we choose with our attention to manifest out of the field in the next moment, and our power and ability to do so relies entirely on what we believe, and on *how we are feeling*.

Brandon West, Creator of Project Global Awakening

This is where quantum physics proves concepts like the Law of Attraction, visualization, prayer, imagery, and "you create your world." This is the Law of Probability. Your act of observing forms your creation, and the energy of your mindset regulates the probability of the creation. In a weird twist of wave physics, this is the equivalent of wave properties: momentum (= level of energy) and amplitude (= probability of creation). This concept is the reason why confidence and intent manifest the intended reality more often than not—the energy of the intent causes a higher likelihood of the event occurring. "Certainty" is one step higher— it is a 100% assured manifestation of the intended event. In this regard the Bible and other religious texts are true when they state, "faith can move mountains."

This also explains why optimists generally create good fortune, and pessimists do not. Their expectation creates an intent, which impacts the probability curve. Think for a moment about the literal meaning of the word "frequency." Literally it means how often an event will occur. When you vibrate at a "frequency" you are fixing the photons of your creation, and the probability that this will occur is the "frequency" you are emitting. Where two or more people are visualizing the same form then the two waves rhythmically entrain, they come together as one wave and amplify, meaning they gain power.

> Everything is energy and that's all there is to it. Match the frequency of the reality you want, and you cannot help but get that reality. It can be no other way. This is not philosophy. This is physics.
> Darryl Anka

You Create Your World

We know our mind is an emitter and receiver of frequencies. What we receive is relative to what we send out. Therefore, be conscious of your thoughts, and guard against negative thoughts, emotions and behaviors. If you are in the "right frame of mind" and are sending out the correct frequencies, you will eventually create whatever it is you are intending. Fear is a powerful attractor; fear creates focused energy and increases the probability of occurrence. 'You attract your fears' is a valid statement.

As you begin to create using the Law of Creation, several things begin to happen, or are reinforced:

- ❖ You impress yourself with your newfound ability. Obviously, you always had the ability, but now you understand how it works, you become better at it.
- ❖ You start to 'un-create'; now that you know the reasons how you create; you begin to choose not to create negative or low-vibrational outcomes.
- ❖ As you create a better crafted life, you naturally display joy. Joy is a higher vibrational emotion. This leads to an upward spiral of emotions. So, as you create, your ability to create increases.
- ❖ Fear no longer reigns supreme. You are no longer wracked by anxiety. Where there was guilt or shame over an event or circumstance, you now choose to correct the event or circumstance. Again, this leads to an upward spiral of emotions.
- ❖ A placebo effect takes place: the more you are in control of what you create, the more you believe in your power to create; "faith has the ability to move mountains".
- ❖ As you create, you distance yourself from your lizard brain and begin to reside in your higher brain.

All these massively increase your potential! But like any art, a process of learning the art or skill leads to an intuitive "knowing" of the art or skill. By following these guidelines, you will have a blueprint to become a Master of the Law of Creation.

Chapter 5 - The Science Behind The Law of Creation

Tracy insisted I separate all the physics stuff into one chapter so that right brained people like her could skip it and get straight to the nuts and bolts of creating. If you are like me, and you need the proof behind this in order to implement it, you might find this as fascinating as I do. This chapter details proof of the Law of Creation. If you are like her, feel free to skip this chapter, as you do not need to know the science behind The Law of Creation in order to make it work for you. But it is fascinating – after all, it is how the Universe was created.

The Physics Behind How We Create Our World

Because of our low level of vibration, and our suggestibility traits, we require 'proof' for a concept to be accepted. This section details a graphic journey through the physics of how we create our world.

Throughout our Universe energy travels in a wave until it hits an interference. Scientists tried to observe the wave. In so doing, the wave became individual photons. **The act of observing changed the energy from a wave to a physical particle**. I highly recommend you watch videos (like Dr. Quantum's Double Slit Experiment) to get a basis for this section, which is the fundamental building block of how we create.

Wave Particle Duality

When the wave hits the interference (the single slit in the Wave Particle Duality diagram), the wave creates a ripple effect on a surface, similar to waves lapping against a shoreline, and the effect is a pattern of photons hitting the wall like the one shown in the following diagram:

Wave Particle Duality

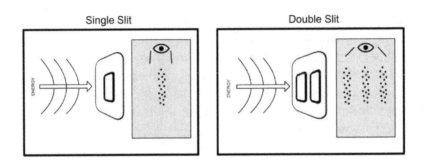

Single Slit   Double Slit

This all fits with our theory of waves. Using a double slit, it was expected that two such patterns would form on the wall. But this was not the case, it formed multiple additional pattern groups. This confounded scientists until they realized that the additional pattern groups were caused by the waves interfering with each other, causing peaks and troughs. The peaks are areas of high frequency, and high probability.

Probability Field

Look at the following Probability Field diagram. In the pattern itself, you can see areas of high and low probability. The part in the middle has a higher 'hit rate' of photons appearing on the surface, in other words, these areas have a higher frequency of occurrence.

Probability Field

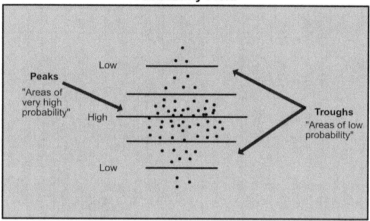

So, through the act of observing, the observer "fixes" the position of the photon. The more focus given by the observer, the higher the probability of a photon appearing in that area. If you practice focus activities such as prayer, imagery, affirmations, etc. then you are increasing the probability of manifesting the photon. The more intensely you focus on a desired outcome, the higher the probability of it occurring. Look at the Probability Infogram that follows; if you have a low level of focus or belief in a particular manifestation, then the probability of it manifesting is reduced, as per the lower left quadrant. But if you have a high level of belief, and/or a high level of focus, then the probability of manifestation surges dramatically, to the point where if you were 100% certain of something, then that manifestation would occur.

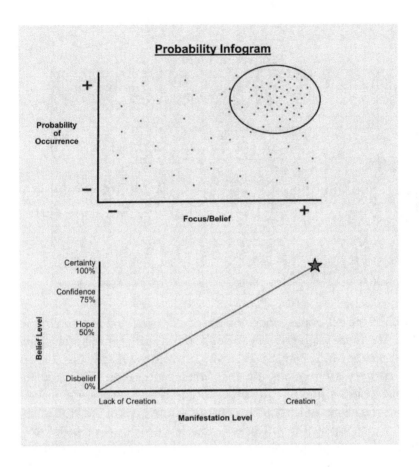

Creation Path

These focusing tools are: desire, thoughts, dreams, mindfulness, imagery, regular affirmations, mass projections like the Maharishi Effect, prayer and gratitude. These are all powerful creational tools which increase the probability of manifestation. Gratitude is the most powerful of these.

Toolbox

Creation Path

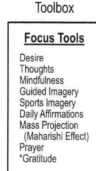

Focus Tools

Desire
Thoughts
Mindfulness
Guided Imagery
Sports Imagery
Daily Affirmations
Mass Projection
    (Maharishi Effect)
Prayer
*Gratitude

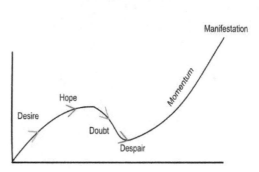

Consider the following Multiverse Theory diagram: when a light wave hits a window some of the light is reflected, some is absorbed by the window, and some light is allowed through. The same thing happens when you observe and "fix" the photons. You absorb or scatter these photons which creates everything you see. This is the world that you create. BUT the wave is also transmitted (transmission) and carries on into the energy field. This leads to a probability field, where anything and everything can be manifested. The energy exists at all stages, and all possible outcomes and manifestations. It is just that, through your act of observing, you have chosen to "fix" the photons at manifestation A, for example, and not manifestation B or C or D, etc. **The wave is pure possibility and the photon/particle is current 'reality'.** I made this bold, because this is the most important concept in this book. **All possible probabilities exist**, but the world you see forms as a direct result of your vibration level which is a result of, and modified by, your thoughts, mood, outlook, programming.

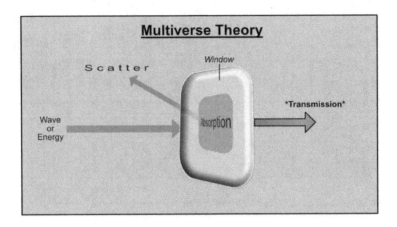

Yet all these probabilities still exist. You have "fixed" the photons and manifested a reality based on your vibration level. This vibration emanates on two levels. The first is your consciousness level. The higher you vibrate, the more of the probability field you can see, and the greater your ability to create alternative manifestations. Like a radio, the messages you receive are based on your receiver.

The second is how dense you are. Energy in a dense matter has a long and slow wavelength (vibrates at a low level), for instance the desk you are sitting at. Energy in a rarefied matter has a short and high wavelength (vibrates at a high level), for instance how light travels though the Universe.

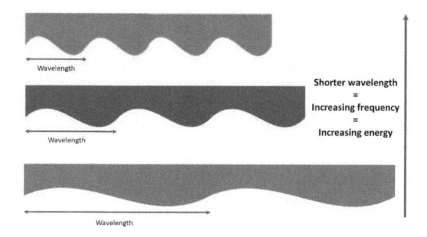

As a human being, your conscious mind is relatively dense; light/energy travels through you relatively slowly, and you vibrate at a relatively low level. Your subconscious mind does not have a physical limitation, is a rarefied matter, and light/energy travels quickly through it (it vibrates at a higher level). So, your conscious mind is only aware of the physical world you see and live in. The subconscious mind sees everything as an energy field, a vibrating Universe, and is able to interact and manipulate that energy.

As per the following Consciousness Understanding Spectrum diagram, if you vibrate at a low level you can only see a limited portion of the probability field (the dark section in the that diagram), in the same way the human eye can only see a tiny portion of the electromagnetic spectrum. If you vibrate at a higher level you can see more of the probability field, and the more able you are to create a manifestation in that enlarged probability field.

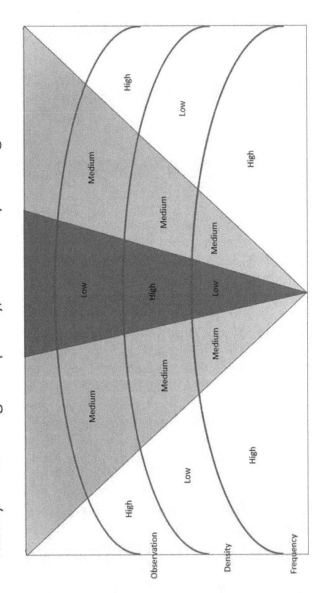

Consciousness Understanding Spectrum

Ideally we have high frequency, low density and high observation

To summarize, what you observe depends on who you are, your level of awareness, whether you are observing with your physical self (conscious mind) or your non-physical self (superconscious mind) which you access through meditation, intuition, pre-cognition, dreams, and Deja-vu. Also important is the fact that the energy you emit is similar to the energy field that you can attract.

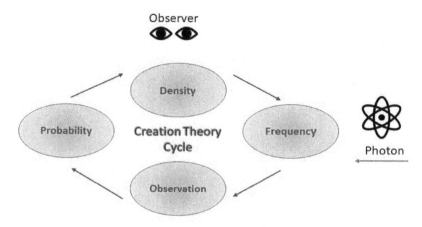

If you have any uncertainty about your ability to create, using your thoughts and locking into the subtle energy of the Universe, then remember this: gravity, magnetism, electricity, dark matter and dark energy are all accepted scientific principles. However, they all share two traits – the first is that we do not understand them; for instance, they go against Newtonian physics in the sense that they never seem to run out of energy. The second is that they are all invisible.

> **To know the mechanics of the wave is to know the entire secret of Nature.**
>
> **Walter Russell**

Duality

In physics terms, a photon is a tiny particle which carries an electromagnetic force. It is the building block of our Universe. But even a humble photon is the epitome of duality. As per Heisenberg's Uncertainty Principle, a photon's momentum OR position can be measured—but not both. Duality at the lowest quantum level of our Universe leads to duality at every level. Hot and cold might seem like opposites, but if you think of them as extremes of temperature, they are not opposite – merely extremes of a single continuum.

Along this continuum is an infinite number of temperatures. The same goes for East and West. If you head far enough West, you end up in a destination that you previously considered as East. This duality is proof that all outcomes exist simultaneously or are potential outcomes in the Field of Probability.

> **Everything is dual; everything has poles; everything has its pair of opposites; like and unlike are the same; opposites are identical in nature but different in degree; extremes meet; all truths are but half-truths; all paradoxes may be reconciled.**
> **The Kybalion**

Quantum Immortality

Based on the infinite probability scenarios postulated by Heisenberg and Schrodinger, and others, all possible outcomes exist at once. This means that there are universes/lives where you died at birth, you died as a youngster (smallpox), you died as a teen (car accident), you died as an adult (cancer). Here's where it gets weirder: the universe/life exists with you as a male/female, red/blonde/black, short/medium/tall, pauper/wealthy/celebrity. Based on the infinite probability scenario you are living all these lives at once—this is the "many worlds interpretation." Think of your cable, satellite, or streaming TV source, how many programs or channels are concurrently being aired? Fifty? Two hundred? One thousand? They are all showing at the same time. Based on how you are feeling, you choose what you want to watch and tune in using your remote. Linking back to "you create your world," you can choose to alter specifics in this current (conscious) life. All these lives are known and acknowledged by your subconscious.

Through focused intent and imagery, we can change our homeostasis re-programming, which prompts the subconscious mind to switch to a different outcome, like changing your TV channel with your remote. Based on the infinite probability scenarios, you never cease to exist—you are always "alive" in some form, infinitely. The atoms in your body are at least 14 billion years old! We know that energy, the source of matter, cannot be created or destroyed, so you are infinitely old. You are infinitely old, in an infinite Universe, in a Field of Infinite Possibilities.

Another way of looking at it is this: consciousness is awareness, awareness of your current body, knowledge and environment. Your focus on a different outcome shifts your awareness to the entity that is "living" that outcome. You become the entity that is consciously aware of the desired outcome. You "experience" the new entity.

Another aspect to consider is time; time is a temporary phenomenon and is completely relative to the observer. If the observer is not there, time does not exist. Time is what ages us and causes our human death. In a non-physical world, time does not exist, and therefore neither does death.

> **Never was there a time when you and I did not exist. Nor will there ever be a time when we cease to exist.**
> **Bhagavad Gita 2:12**

Take Back Your Power

The famous double slit experiment, referenced above, proved to the world that light is both a wave, and a particle, and is therefore quantum in nature. Therefore, it has multiple opposing qualities, simultaneously. The most amazing aspect of this experiment is that it indicates the light photon "chooses" to be a wave or a particle, depending only on whether or not it is being observed. Only observation, or measurement (of its speed or position) manifests its position and state. Heisenberg's Uncertainty Principle states that the more precisely the position of some particle is determined, the less precisely its momentum can be known, and vice versa.

John Wheeler was a theoretical physicist whose "delayed choice experiments" suggest that once a particle passes through the slits it can seem to retroactively alter its previous behavior at the slits. Wheeler concluded that "no phenomenon is a phenomenon until it is an observed phenomenon," and that the Universe does not " . . . exist, out there, independent of all acts of observation."

What little we know about quantum physics implies that the observer creates the reality. Intuitively we know this to be true, even if we do not understand the physical laws of how it is achieved. You, the observer, have the power to create your environment and existence. By accepting that you are responsible for where you are in your life, without shame, blame or judgment, you start to take back your creative powers. For as long as you hold somebody or some event responsible for where you are in life, or your suffering, you deny your creative powers. Consciousness Engineering, covered in Chapter 7, explores this concept in detail.

Chapter 6 - Increase Your Potential, The Tools of the Trade

We are all born with a script. This is a summation of our experiences, values, and beliefs. Typically, we will only rise to the level of the script we have been programmed with. Yet we have an amazing ability to rewrite that script, to increase our worthiness, our expectations and our *deservability*! There are proven ways to increase our success, prosperity and happiness.

Henry Ford said, "Whether you think you can, or think you can't, you are right." This statement is brilliant in its simplicity and underlines the creative power we all have, but the quote is wrong in one area. "Think you can" implies it is a conjecture of the conscious mind. Change this to "know you can." So, a truer statement is "whether you know you can, or know you can't, you are right!" When the subconscious mind accepts something as real, it will manifest the reality.

> **Do, or do not. There is no try!**
> **Yoda**

The Power of Words and Thought

Everything about you is electromagnetic. Each cell in your body, each organ, fiber, vessel, muscle and bone has an electromagnetic vibration. Your brain has a high electromagnetic vibration, only surpassed by your heart. Each thought you have has an electromagnetic vibration, as does every word you say. As you know, electromagnetic energy has a magnetic force. Each of your thoughts attracts or repels events and experiences in line with your vibration level. Who you are, how you think, and how you act all create the manifestation that you *attract*.

Towards the end of the 20th century researchers learned that the hypothalamus transforms a thought—or meme—into millions of neuropeptides that represent the emotion of a thought. For every experience of thought, the brain's "control center" releases a storm of amino acids into the bloodstream, which then insert themselves into cells within the brain-body system. And, over time, these cells begin to crave these particular neuropeptides, creating a self-fulfilling prophecy of emotion. Now, scientists find that negative thoughts not only affect mood but also other aspects of physical health and increasing levels of inflammation in the body associated with a number of disorders and conditions.

Water memory illustrates how our thoughts and intentions can alter our physical world. This has been amply demonstrated through studies on water by Dr. Masaru Emoto, which studies show how intentions and thought shape the way water crystallizes. Dr. Emoto conducted many experiments whereby he put water into containers and pasted a word or words onto the containers. After a period of time, the water was frozen, and the crystals were examined under an electron microscope. The water associated with "pleasant" words formed beautiful crystals. Those with "bad" words formed misshapen and ugly crystals. The inference here is that the energy of the word impacted on the water, either positively or negatively, and Dr. Emoto stated that: "We all hold a certain vibrational frequency, and our bodies are estimated to be about 70% water. Given the above experiments, it stands to reason that musical frequencies could also alter our own vibrational state. Every expression through sound, emotion, or thought holds a specific frequency which influences everything around it—much like a single drop of water can create a larger ripple effect in a large body of water."

Interestingly, Dr. Masaru Emoto found that the most perfectly formed crystal was with the words "Love and Gratitude." Not "Love" on its own, nor "Gratitude"—these are beautiful crystals, but not as perfect as Love *and* Gratitude. He surmised from this that "Love and Gratitude" has a higher vibration than either of the words on its own: a case of "the whole is more than the sum of its parts." Note the perfectly formed crystal below is entitled "Love and Thanks", and the malformed crystal is "You Fool":

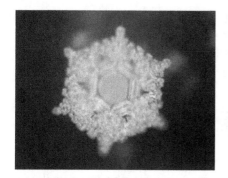
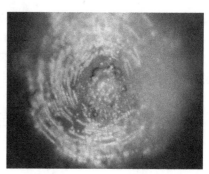

"Love and Thanks"   "You Fool"

Your thoughts and words underline the energy transfer from you, to the water in your body, which affects your blood, cells, brain and organs.

Energy carries information. Recent studies prove that water flowing in a river had more 'information' at the river mouth than at its source. Somehow it had "'acquired" information along the way. So, your thoughts have powerful information which you transfer to your body (and the Universe). It is a two-way street—everything you come into contact with transfers information to you, and you to it.

It may take time for you to realize the impact of your thinking; to help you grasp this concept think of your subconscious mind as a bank – whatever you deposit will grow and will earn compound interest. Deposit thoughts of prosperity, wealth, success, love, joy and gratitude. And know that when you have thoughts of fear, anger, doubt, anxiety – then you are making a withdrawal from your account.

> **Until you make the unconscious conscious, it will direct your life –**
> **and you will call it fate.**
> **Carl Jung**

Once you implement positive thinking, your world becomes rapidly and positively transformed. What you think is what you become. We know with quantum physics that you, the Observer, create reality from chaos. You, the Observer, are the Creator of your world, your universe. I am pretty sure that you try your best with everything you do in life. In which case, why not choose to create a perfect existence?

Visualizing the Outcome

When you visualize something in your mind, your mind-body responds as if it is real. For instance, if I visualize myself walking the dog, the brain creates chemicals and the muscles react electrically as if I were actually walking the dog. The subconscious brain does not know the difference between real and imagined. The more you imagine, the more real you make it – in two ways: firstly, the body believes it, and secondly you are increasing the frequency (probability of it occurring) as explained in Chapter 5.

The more you visualize the event, and the more senses you involve, and the more emotion you involve – the greater the probability of the event transpiring.

Homeostasis

Another important aspect is that of homeostasis - the desire for things to stay the same. The subconscious mind hates unknowns and our inherent efficiency keeps us using the same neural pathways. In general, humans dislike change, as change takes us out of our comfort zone, so in everything we do we tend to stick to the same habits, routines and patterns. This keeps us "stuck" at the level of our script. In order to change your homeostasis, you can harness four tools:

1. Be open to all possibilities, and allow yourself to set the bar higher, dream of bigger things, have a sense of self-worth, and come to "believe" in the new script.
2. Use daily reinforcement of all the tools and tips described in this book. We know that a key Law of Creation is repetition.
3. Your subconscious brain works with symbolic language. For instance, you can use the $ symbol not only to indicate wealth and abundance, but also as a symbol to signify your increased joy, love, peace, etc.

4. Pick a specific time of day to manifest your new reality, to do your affirmations, and to practice gratitude. A good time is just before sleep—because of the Alpha state you drift into, the gate to your subconscious is already open.

Fear as a Creation Disruptor

What you resist, will persist. You are giving energy to negative things. Focus only on what you want, not on what you do not want. When I learned to ride a motorcycle I was cautioned to focus on where I wanted to go and not the pothole in the road, for if you focus on the pothole, guess what happens? When you focus on what you do not want, you are accidentally vibrating at that frequency. Frequency becomes probability.

Worry and fear is 'unbelief'. Unbelief is actually belief in the opposite of what we desire to create. Or is it? Behind every fear is a wish. Fear is a creative tool – but sadly it tends to create the opposite of what we had hoped for. When conflicting beliefs exist, we sabotage our reality creation. That is why we fail to manifest what we want.

Worrying is using your imagination and emotion to create something you do not want. Worry and fear is unbelief. Our beliefs create reality. When conflicting beliefs exist, we sabotage our reality creation. That is why we fail to manifest what we want. Start to feel good about what you want, speak right about what you want, (for example when you don't want to **forget** to take the trash out, tell yourself to **remember** to take the trash out, instead of telling yourself not to forget as the subconscious mind does not deal with negatives - "**don't** forget" versus "remember to"), take action towards what you want. When all thought, feeling, words and actions are in alignment, your desire will manifest a lot faster and more completely. Being out of alignment in any one of these areas always impedes your manifestation in some form. Like water in a river, energy takes the easiest path. Electric current uses the shortest path to flow. Therefore, offer a path by thinking and visualizing what you want.

As per the Multiverse Theory diagram in Chapter 5, some light always carries on into the Field of Probability. When you shift your focus onto the possibilities, you increase the frequency of probability. If you focus on your current life and situation, then this is what you will manifest more of. By focusing on an alternative, that is what you will manifest. For instance, 'depression' – it may seem that I am simplifying depression, but I'm not - when a person is in a depressed state that person tends to focus on what is wrong - the current down side of your life as it exists right now; not only does this cement into reality the features of that life, it also shuts down creativity (imagining, visualizing, hoping), making it harder to move out of depression. By shifting your focus, you not only change what you are manifesting, you also begin to change your depressed state. It can be that easy! Fear is equally inefficient as you focus on what you do not want to happen (like hitting the pothole), but the focus itself is creating the unwanted issue and increasing the frequency of probability. If you focus on your fears and unwanted situations, then this is what you will manifest.

Fear of Failure

The fear of failure is so common it even has its own "phobia" name— atychiphobia. A person may have a clearly defined goal which they want to achieve. But this can be offset by an unclear, subconscious goal. For example, think of a person wanting to deliver a public speech. Their conscious goal is a well-delivered address to a public audience. However, the fear of failing - making a fool of themselves or forgetting what they want to say, is present in their mind. So, the vision of an entertained audience hanging on their every word is one goal and the vision of being laughed at is a different and opposite goal. Your brain does not differentiate between whether what you want is good or bad, it just delivers what you think about through a cycle of selective attention, action and reinforcement.

You can operate daily out of Love or Fear. Love is an attractor; Fear is a repellant, and in terms of the Law of Creation, it is a 'bank account withdrawal'. Like the previous example of reminding yourself to take the trash out, telling yourself to remember to take the trash out is the positive manifestation, while telling yourself not to forget is the negative – the subconscious does not deal with negatives and **don't** is negative in this case so all your subconscious hears is "forget", it does not hear "don't".

Fear of Success

Fear of success is similar to fear of failure. They have many of the same symptoms, and both fears hold us back from achieving our dreams and goals.

If you have been programmed to believe that you are only worth 'x', then it will be impossible to reach a value of '2x'. Your homeostasis is a powerful belief system which brings about manifestation – what you deeply believe, you will manifest. If you subconsciously believe that you do not deserve to be successful, then you will create exactly that: a lack of success.

Some people will not attempt to succeed because when they fail it emphasizes what they believed in the first place – that they are a failure. Not attempting something means that there is no blatant proof that they are a failure. So, in their heads, they could be anything they want to be if only they wanted to be. This fantasy would be dashed by attempting to acquire success and not achieving it, and this would then be evidence that they are a failure.

This single aspect separates successful people from unsuccessful people: a person who believes in themselves will attempt something wherein they do not know if they will succeed but a) they are optimistic that they can succeed, and b) if they fail they have enough self-esteem or self-belief to accept the failure and then analyze the failure so that they can learn the lesson and use this experience in the next venture. A pessimist, or a person with low self-esteem will not try to succeed because a) their belief that it will fail or b) lack of belief in themselves.

Affirmations

Affirmations refer primarily to the practice of positive thinking and self-empowerment—fostering a belief that "a positive mental attitude supported by affirmations will achieve success in anything." More specifically, an affirmation is a carefully formatted statement that should be written down and repeated to oneself frequently. For an affirmation to be effective, it needs to be present tense, positive, personal and specific. Said out loud also increases their effectiveness.

The word affirmation comes from the Latin *affirmare*, originally meaning "to make steady, strengthen." And that is what it does to our lives—it steadies and strengthens us, our mind, our body, and our beliefs.

Affirmations are proven methods of self-improvement because of their ability to rewire our brains, by creating a path to our subconscious. Similar to exercise, they allow the release of feel-good hormones which our brains use to form new clusters of "positive thought" neurons in the sequence of thought-speech-action, affirmations play an integral role by breaking patterns of negative thoughts, negative speech, and, in turn, negative actions.

Essentially, we really do create our world. What we reflect, what we think and say and do, becomes our reality. Dr. Masaru Emoto's work on water crystals reveals the effect energy has on water. As we are over 70% water, this energy also has a massive effect on our bodies and minds. Thus, what you think is what you become.

A powerful daily activity is the saying of affirmations to yourself. These affirmations help you to:
- vibrate at a higher level
- attract the outcome you are describing
- start to move you up the emotional spiral
- focus on what it is that you desire in life

> **Every thought we think is creating our future.**
> **Louise Hay**

Remember to repeat your affirmation(s) often enough that it becomes a mantra of your life. Be as specific as you can and ***believe*** in the affirmation! It is your belief that brings about the manifestation. Without belief, affirmations are just words.

Dr. Bruce Lipton (in "7 Ways to Reprogram Your Mind") states, "Your subconscious beliefs are working either for you or against you, but the truth is that you are not controlling your life, because your subconscious mind supersedes all conscious control. So, when you are trying to heal from a conscious level—citing affirmations and telling yourself you're healthy—there may be an invisible subconscious program that's sabotaging you."

The simple reason affirmations do or do not work, is whether or not your subconscious "believes" the affirmation. Repetition is a good way to program your subconscious—continual exposure to something makes it a "truth" over time.

The most powerful affirmations are those that create images in the subconscious. As you state your affirmation, VISUALIZE the end result in your mind. See yourself as BEING 25 lbs. lighter, see you DRIVING your new car, PICTURE the check for $1M (in detail – who is the check from? Date? Signed by?). And focus on the feelings! How would you feel if you had a check for $1M in your hand right now? The subconscious mind works in symbols and images, not language. You need to affirm in emotions, symbols and images.

A current affirmation of Tracy's is: "Each and every day I see the beauty in this world and connect with others in love." The way Tracy developed this and other affirmations was to look at the description of the emotions (covered in the next chapter under Power versus Force) and choose how she wanted to live the rest of her life, how she wanted to feel and what she wanted to achieve and developed the affirmations accordingly to help her reach this level of emotion. Tracy resonated with Joy which vibrates at a level of 540. The characteristics of Joy are "unconditional love and a permanent feeling of joy. Each moment is bliss. People vibrating with joy display unwavering belief and patience despite massive trials and tribulations. They are consumed by compassion for the world and everything in it. They see the world as a place of peace, beauty and happiness (because these are manifested from within). They are capable of manifesting high-level events, and even miracles." Tracy has the affirmations pasted to her bathroom mirror, so she sees them first thing in the morning and last thing at night.

Handwriting

Your handwriting flows from your subconscious—it tells us about your state of mind. There are several aspects of handwriting which relate to improving your self-esteem and self-worth. Your handwriting is an ideo-motor process. If you were to write out a full page of cursive writing, on a blank page with no lines, your writing gives good clues and signals as to your emotional, physical, physiological and psychological state. Interestingly, the reverse is true. By learning and applying specific handwriting traits, we train and lead our subconscious.

For example, the height of your "t" represents your ego/self-esteem. The height of the bar on the "t" is your confidence level, or your goals. A high bar indicates high confidence or ambitious goals. The width of the bar indicates drive for success—our ability to start projects, follow through, and finish them. If you now start doing tall "t's" with a high crossbar, and a wide crossbar, you will subconsciously acquire more self-esteem, confidence, and resourcefulness in finishing projects. See the insert for an example of Thomas Edison's t's—they are impressive!

Graphology is outside the scope of this book, but for any reader interested in taking this further I recommend a handwriting analysis course. In the meantime, practice rewriting your "t's"—you now have tall "t's" with a long bar placed high up on the stem!

The Power of Group Consciousness / Prayer

Thoughts emanate from you in a wave pattern. Where several people combine their thoughts (e.g. a prayer group) the waves form peaks and troughs. The peaks bring about an increased probability of manifesting the event being prayed for, an increased frequency of the event. Intense prayer or supplication by an individual also harnesses this effect. The Maharishi Effect is caused by this phenomenon. Energy waves have two values: frequency and amplitude. The frequency is the nature of your thoughts and desires, the amplitude is the power or intensity of those thoughts and desires. Group consciousness and intense prayer are both ways to increase the amplitude (power).

Reality Imagery

Thinking about how you want that creation to look like is only semi-effective. The most powerful way to create is to act as if it was already there. Act as if you are a billionaire, act as if you are a transcended master, act as if you are at the top of your profession, etc. Your old creation process of "think, say, act"' should be turned around—it now becomes "act, say, think." Ordinarily, if you were a billionaire, you could give freely of your wealth to other people. You might not have liquid cash to give, but you can give abundance to others in whatever means you have available to you. For instance, give of yourself—give time and attention to others who need your experience and wisdom.

The Brainwave State Paradox

Every second of the day, each neuron and synapse in our brain is firing with electrical energy. This constant flow of electrical energy ensures fluid communication from the brain to the body, from the body to the brain, and between the various parts of the brain. It can be measured by an electroencephalography device, which is commonly known as an EEG. We measure this cyclical energy in Hertz (cycles per second). Varying states of emotional behavior trigger varying states of electrical energy within our brains. We call these "brainwave states," and the following are their main ranges:

Brainwave	Hertz Range	Behavior
Epsilon	0.5 and	
Delta	0.5 to 4.5	Deep natural sleep. Sleep induced by drugs or substances.
Theta	4.5 to 7.5	Light sleep, REM sleep, dreaming, deep hypnosis, emotions such as gratitude.
Alpha	7.5 to 12.5	Deep relaxation, moments before falling asleep or waking, basic meditation, mindfulness, light hypnosis.
Beta	12.5 to 30	Normal 'awake' state
Gamma and Hyper Gamma	30 to 60 60 to 100	'Fight or flight', 'in the zone', terror, shock, extreme excitement, euphoria.
Lambda	100 and	

Epsilon (<0.5Hz)—This brain frequency range was only recently 'discovered' and is still very controversial. I call this the 'God state'.

Delta (0.5 Hz to 4 Hz)—This brain frequency range is where the body is in its deepest sleep, healing, and rejuvenating itself. Generally, a person is unconscious in this state. A person in a coma would be in a deep Delta state, 1Hz for example.

Theta (4 Hz to 7.5 Hz)—In light (REM) sleep, and deep meditation, our brain is in theta state. A person in theta can also experience a deep connection to source, profound insights, and visualizations.

Alpha (7.5 Hz to 12.5 Hz)—When we are very relaxed, about to drift off to sleep, daydreaming, traveling without consciously remembering the route—these are all performed in this state. It is also associated with intuitive thinking, insight, creativity, and deep relaxation.

Beta (12.5 Hz to 30 Hz)—Beta brainwaves are the typical state when we are awake, and our general mental awareness when actively engaged in the world. In this state, the physical senses are alert and actively taking in information.

Gamma (30 Hz to 60 Hz, usually around 40 Hz)—Gamma brainwaves are associated with higher mental functioning, anxiety, being "in the zone", and peak concentration.

Lambda (100Hz+) – This brain frequency range was only recently 'discovered' and is still very controversial.

As the above table shows, the mind is at different wavelengths depending on our state, emotions, nutrition, and external factors. All of these brainwaves are active in our brain all of the time, but one of the brainwave states will be the most dominant—and again this depends on the person; how they are feeling/experiencing, what they are busy doing, the time of day and what their emotions are.

Alpha state and lower allows access to the subconscious. The Law of Intensity states that the strength of any memory is proportional to the strength of emotion at the time of the memory. So, for any new behavior to become cemented into the subconscious, it requires a high-level brainwave state—like Gamma for instance. This leads to a paradox—if the relaxed Alpha state opens the subconscious, and the intense Gamma state "burns" the memory into the subconscious, surely the two brainwave states cannot coexist?

Typically, one of these two scenarios occur:

❖ We wake up, and in a Beta state enact Law of Creation protocols such as affirmation and gratitude. We can accompany this with a burst of feel-good emotion (Gamma state).

❖ As we drift off to sleep (Alpha state) we enact Law of Creation protocols such as affirmation and gratitude. We can accompany this with a feel-good intention (Beta state).

But as mentioned above, the key is to use Alpha state to open the subconscious and Gamma state to "burn" it into the subconscious.

One method to achieve this "dual" brainwave state is using binaural beats, whereby we can introduce any brainwave frequency to the brain (within reason). So, in theory we could be in a state of hypnosis (Alpha state) and receive a binaural beat of 30 Hz+ (Gamma state).

A second method is when the body is profoundly relaxed and the mind is in a state of high focus and concentration, both low (10 Hz) and high (40 Hz) brain activity can be seen in the EEG of some subjects.

But the most powerful method is this: gratitude can be a thought, or it can be deeply felt, energized by amplified emotion. Gratitude is a theta brainwave state—when this gratitude is deeply felt it receives a dose of Gamma. Gamma is seen in blessings and euphoria. A deep state of gratitude is a combination of blessings and euphoria—giving blessings for your positive state combined with a sense of euphoria because of your positive state. Simply put, gratitude is the most powerful method of manifesting your intentions.

It is believed that Tibetan monks meditating achieve Gamma state. Perhaps the years of dedicated training allow the mind to be in an Alpha state, whilst the mind-body achieves a Gamma state. Ironically, their power of manifestation probably allows them to manifest anything they want, but their level of consciousness means that they don't want for anything. Like the balance in nature, Gamma has both a negative aspect (it is the state of fear, stress and anxiety) and an opposite positive aspect (focus, performance, memory, compassion).

The Grand Plan / Soul Contract

Sometimes a desired outcome only manifests much later, and in other cases it never does at all. Let's say, for instance, you desire the highest possible outcome for you—let's choose "a venture that is meaningful and that earns a plentiful income." You are then surprised and disappointed when your next venture fails, and the one after that. Finally, perhaps many years later, you launch a venture which succeeds, and fills you with happiness. The two (or more) failures were required to help you understand what you do like, and what you don't like. One venture may have been profitable, but not meaningful, and perhaps the other meaningful but not profitable.   Hopefully, the resulting successful venture gives you the sense of purpose you require, while at the same time earns the income you were hoping for. Have patience, have belief, and trust in the path that you are on. After all, you created the path, and you chose the route. Trust in yourself. Absorb the feedback from each thought, action, and venture, and adjust the wind in your sails.

If, for example, you want to attract abundant wealth into your life and are consciously trying to manifest it, but your soul contract was to experience scarcity and poverty, there is a paradox. Our soul contract is subconscious, and our Law of Creation mantras are conscious. We know our subconscious is many times more powerful than our conscious—in which case, which one do you think will send a stronger signal to the Universe? If our goal in life is to find and achieve ascendancy through consciousness, and we recognize that most Law of Creation requests we make are for material things in our life, then we can appreciate that this is incongruent. The bottom line is take care of your **needs**, and not your **wants**.

Focus on What You Really, Really Want

Let's say you want to manifest tons of money. Ask yourself why? Why do you want lots of money? Perhaps it is not the money you want, maybe it is the freedom, independence and choice that having the money presents. Rather, then, focus on the end result: in this case the freedom, the independence and the choice that you crave. I would like to point out here the topic of 'wishing'. Wishing is in fact a negative process. It is motivated by fear. Associated with the wish is the awareness of 'lack'. The awareness that you lack the money, the health, or whatever you are wishing for. Also, when you wish for something, it is an indication that you do not expect the wish to materialize, otherwise you would not have wished for it in the first place. Wishing also lacks the "enthused emotions". Remember the Law of Creation formula? **Visualization + Enthused Emotion = Manifestation**

Do Not Be Attached to the Outcome

You've probably heard this multiple times— "do not be attached to the outcome." Obviously, this is strange because you desire a particular outcome, and this is why it is a desire. What it really means is this: do not *fear* the outcome, or the outcome might not manifest. Design an outcome, set your intent, and let it manifest. If it did not manifest, do not be concerned. Merely re-set the intent. Through continuous belief (Laws of Repetition, Perception, Belief, and Probability), your subconscious starts to understand your design.

Religious Belief

What you perceive as reality, is reality. Some people believe fully in religious texts, such as the Bible. Using elements from these texts is a powerful reinforcement. One example is the Gospel of Mark in the New Testament: "What things so ever ye desire, when ye pray, believe that ye receive them and ye shall receive them." Interestingly this statement underlines the Reality Imagery and Law of Perception/Belief already discussed. If you believe in the power of prayer, for instance, this lends power to the probability of the prayer being answered. The physics behind this is explained in Chapter 5. In essence, the more we believe something to be true, the more probable it becomes.

The Power of Gratitude

The power of gratitude is threaded throughout this book. In terms of the Law of Creation, it is the single most powerful element. For instance, when you state affirmations, consider the following: Each and every day my body is in perfect health. Or, Each and every day **I AM GRATEFUL** that my body is in perfect health.

The second affirmation is many times more powerful than the first especially if you add the enthused emotion of gratitude. With any affirmation use present tense ("I am..." as opposed to "I hope..." or "I desire..." or "I will...") and "I am grateful that..." or "thankful for...". We see from Dr. Masaru Emoto's work on water crystals, and the beauty of the crystals associated with "Love and Gratitude" that when combined, these words are far more powerful than "Love" or "Gratitude" on their own. Despite this, "Gratitude" is one of the most powerful forces in the world. When applying the Law of Creation, know that gratitude is a powerful amplifier.

Gratitude is an emotion expressing appreciation for what one has—as opposed to an emphasis on what one wants. When you express gratitude for what you have, the Universe reacts and manifests more of what you are grateful for.

I once attended a seminar by Dr. John Demartini and he related the following story: Demartini has a billionaire friend who, when he asked how he became a billionaire, replied: "Every night I run through all the events of the day, giving gratitude for everything. In the beginning it took a long time, but now it takes me five minutes every evening." In effect this billionaire works for five minutes a day. The good vibrations his gratitude creates attract the experiences and events that make him a billionaire.

So, ask yourself—do you want to toil endlessly for eight or more hours, every day, to make a living, or does it make sense to take a short time during the day to do a gratitude meditation?

In the previous chapter I refer to homeostasis, the natural levels of your emotions and success script in your subconscious. There are several ways to improve this script, to reprogram it. One of the ways is constant gratitude. The Law of Creation argues that thoughts are energy. Gratitude is a thought energized with a strong amplifying emotion.

According to Chuck Danes in www.abundance-and-happiness.com "When you are in a sincere state of gratitude your energy (vibrational resonance) is one of acceptance and harmony. You resonate, and as a result project a much higher vibrational frequency which is exactly what attracts to you the events, conditions, and circumstances that you desire. In other words, enabling, and allowing, yourself to transition into and remain in a state of gratitude puts you in harmonious alignment while, concurrently, this emits and projects a vibrational resonance which attracts additional energies of the same kind and quality as the projected, deeply felt, emotion of gratitude."

> **Whatever we think about and thank about we bring about**
>
> **John Demartini**

Many current studies show that we can mentally and deliberately manufacture a culture of gratitude and appreciation. Our overall well-being and happiness increases by doing so.

Previously, I referred to how powerful gratitude is for the Law of Creation: *A deep state of gratitude is a combination of blessings and euphoria—giving blessings for your positive state combined with a sense of euphoria because of your positive state. Simply put, gratitude is the most powerful method of manifesting your intentions.*

> **The way to move out of judgement is to move into gratitude**
>
> **Neale Donald Walsch**

Chapter 7 – What is Consciousness?

We are Consciousness Engineers

What has consciousness got to do with your ability to create? The simple answer is ... everything!

At its root, consciousness is a holistic concept describing our experience of life on Earth, and our attempt to interpret it in terms of emotion and intellectual thought—who are we, who am I in relation to who you are, where do we come from, where are we going to, what are we supposed to do here on Earth, and what is the purpose of our existence on Earth? When we are born, we are not given a "how to . . ." guide; we are spiritual beings in a human avatar, conducting fantasy role-play in a quantum mechanics world!

> **My life is a story of the self-realization of the unconscious.**
>
> **Carl Jung**

The mind is responsible for our level of functioning, achievement and happiness. This chapter will establish that each of us has several minds. Disease, dysfunction and behavioral disorder manifest in our lower minds—the Primitive Mind and the Emotional Mind—they cannot manifest at the level of the Higher Mind, which is linked to our higher consciousness and emotions. Through raising our consciousness and emotions, we can vibrate at a higher level and thereby attain a high level of functioning, success, health and happiness.

The way our different brains are responsible for our different behavioral functioning is explored in this chapter. I believe that everybody is a consciousness engineer—in which case an understanding of consciousness is a fundamental necessity.

This chapter also explores concepts such as Hawkins' Power versus Force, and Hicks' Emotional Scale which graphically explain the levels of consciousness. This allows all of us to 'measure' where we are on the scale of consciousness. Our ability to create is inextricably linked to our level of consciousness. If we know where we stand on this scale, we can better understand our limitations and abilities to create. In addition, it explains concepts such as the human brain as a transmitter and receiver of signals, left brain versus right brain consciousness, "inter-connectedness" of everything, and "what we believe to be true is created by us individually."

> **Every part of your body has its own consciousness or its own soul.**
>
> **Anon/Indigenous Medicine Healers**

When you consider the three areas of the brain, note that the higher brain is linked to higher consciousness:

- ❖ the reptilian brain, command center for reflexes and instincts
- ❖ the mammalian brain, command center for emotions
- ❖ the higher brain (neocortex), command center for logical and abstract thinking

	BRAIN	PURPOSE	ABILITY	BRAINWAVE STATE
Higher Self	Higher Brain (Neo-Cortex)	Awareness	Logical Thinking Abstract Thinking	Alpha
Ego	Mammalian Brain (Limbic System)	Emotions	Behavior Long Term Memory	Beta
	Reptilian Brain (Amygdala)	Self-Preservation	Reflexes Instinct Base Needs (Hunger, Sex)	Gamma

(Consciousness increases upward)

The higher brain allows a higher level of actions, as opposed to base level needs. Mindfulness and meditation are two ways we can move the focus to a higher mind and away from primitive reactive behaviors.

Parts of the reptilian brain vibrate at a low level, such as autonomic functions like breathing and digestion that take place whilst we are in deep sleep. But reptilian emotions are all high Beta to Gamma wave states: anger, fight-and-flight, lust, fear, terror, aggression, stress, anxiety, etc.

Many brilliant people have stated that the matter we see around us was created by us, through our consciousness:

❖ Erwin Schrödinger: "Consciousness cannot be accounted for in physical terms. For consciousness is absolutely fundamental. It cannot be accounted for in terms of anything else."
❖ Nikola Tesla: "The day science begins to study non-physical phenomena; it will make more progress in one decade that in all of the previous centuries of its existence."
❖ Max Planck: "I regard consciousness as fundamental. I regard matter as derivative from consciousness. We cannot get behind consciousness. Everything that we talk about, everything that we regard as existing, postulates consciousness."
❖ Eugene Wigner: "It [is] not possible to formulate the laws of quantum mechanics in a fully consistent way without reference to consciousness."

This means that the individual you, and the collective us, all create the world around us. This is immensely powerful: if you have created an environment which you wish to change then according to the rules of consciousness you have the power to change it.

All consciousness seems to be entheogenic—manifesting the God within. Whether you believe there is a supreme God whose rules we have to follow to become like that God, or you believe quantum physics in suggesting we have created our complete world and environment—and therefore we are "God"— the purpose of consciousness seems to become more "God-like."

We know through the Laws of Entropy that the macroscopic world is absolute chaos. We assemble and bring order through our act of observation. Our observation brings about the reality that we see.

Your **conscious** mind vibrates at a certain level and so transmits and receives messages and events at this level. Your **subconscious** mind vibrates at a certain level and so transmits and receives messages and events at this level (notably a higher level). Because the two minds are on different frequencies (the subconscious at a higher vibration) they cannot transmit and receive to each other. When you are in your conscious mind, you cannot access your subconscious process (try and switch off all the cells in your right hand, for example). When you are in your subconscious mind, you cannot access your conscious process (while sleeping, for example).

Meditation, by way of example, quietens the conscious mind and allows cognitive transfer to the subconscious. During the period of meditation, you reconnect with your source, receive programming from it, and feel generally happier. This is why meditation is effective—you temporarily reduce the obstructive and low-vibrating conscious mind (aka the ego).

Consciousness is not a one-person thing, even though we experience it from a one-person perspective. Consciousness is all-encompassing. Evidence of group consciousness is present everywhere. The Maharishi Effect is an example: "In 1974 in eleven cities in the USA, when the number of people participating in the Transcendental Meditation Program (TMP) reached one per cent of the city population, the trend of rising crime rate was seen to be reversed, indicating increasing order and harmony in the life of the whole city. The research scientists named this phenomenon, of rising coherence in the collective consciousness of the whole society through the practice of TMP, the Maharishi Effect (Maharishi Mahesh Yogi, predicted this effect as early as 1960). Research involving several hundred other cities subsequently replicated this original finding."
Source: http://maharishi-programmes.globalgoodnews.com/maharishi-effect/research.html

Supposedly the individuals experience and enliven the field of Transcendental Consciousness—the experience of the Unified Field of

Natural Law. When a sufficient number of individuals enliven this field, then through a "Field Effect" of consciousness (the Maharishi Effect) an influence of orderliness and harmony is radiated from the level of the Unified Field of Natural Law to the whole population.

Buddhism recognizes eight types of consciousness. The first five are those of the eye, ear, body, nose and tongue, our human senses. The sixth is the conceptualizing mind, our conscious mind. The seventh, called *manas*, is the subconscious. The eighth, called *alaya*, is the superconscious.

In our current world perspective, consciousness is the act of self-observing. Where we self-observe and make positive adjustments, our consciousness 'grows'. Where we take no action, our consciousness regresses or stays the same (inertia).

My definition of consciousness is this: humans are simple animals responding to chemical signals. These chemical signals make us react without due thought. When we recognize this, and start to discern the signals, this allows us to act, think and proceed in a more powerful manner; we are no longer slaves to chemical urges, we can now apply sentient thought which leads to better defined outcomes. Continued practice of this self-reflection ultimately leads to inner discoveries about who we are, where we came from, and where we are going to. Personally, I think this might even be the way to ascendancy, where we can separate from the mundane low-vibrating constraints of the Earth we reside on.

> **Between stimulus and response there is space.**
> **In that space is our power to choose our response.**
> **In our response lies our growth and our freedom.**
> **Attributed to Viktor Frankl**

"Oneness" and Emotions

In 1966 a famous experiment was performed by Cleve Backster – an interrogation specialist for the CIA. Backster had studied plants from the early 1960s. In February 1966 he was experimenting with a plant, when he came across a unique finding.

Backster had connected a Dracaena cane plant to a polygraph, to measure the time taken for root water to reach the leaves, and noticed readings on the polygraph responded to his thoughts about the leaf. For instance, when he thought about burning the leaf, the polygraph went wild. The plant registered a stress response to his malicious thoughts! He then conducted further experiments, testing the plant's response to various emotional scenarios. He deduced that plants perceive human intentions and that human thoughts and emotions cause reactions in them that can be measured by a polygraph instrument. He ascertained that plants react to human thoughts and published his findings in a book called "Primary Perception". Based on subsequent experiments, he later claimed "primary perception" could be measured in all living things. Many similar experiments have been performed proving this amazing concept.

These experiments were perhaps the first of their kind to demonstrate "inter-connectedness" between everything. Buddhism, most Eastern religions, and many spiritual modalities, encompass the concept of oneness. As humans, we tend only to believe what we can see. Because we cannot see this "oneness" we deny its existence. But modern science is providing irrefutable proof of it.

In quantum physics, entangled particles, even when separated by great distances, remain connected so that actions performed on one particle have an immediate and automatic effect on the other. This is the phenomenon that Einstein called "Spooky action at a distance." There are many 'weird' rules in quantum physics, but the primary one is that "an unobserved photon exists in all possible states simultaneously but, when observed or measured, exhibits only one state". The typical experiment splits photons into "entangled pairs." If the one photon spins in a clockwise fashion, then the other will spin in an anticlockwise motion. Whatever action performed on the one photon, the other photon imitates, but in an opposite way. Not only does this show inter-connectedness, but it also demonstrates the concept of balance—for each and every action there is an equal and opposite reaction. Even matter has anti-matter—at the basest level of energy there exists balance and duality. Take note that these photons could be separated by vast distances and still behave the same way. It also emphasizes the duality of our Universe.

Current science has no explanation, or rules, that might govern these phenomena. But modern science has always struggled to explain key unknowns. Gravity and magnetism are two more unexplainable phenomena that defy Newtonian physics. The edge of the Universe is currently calculated at 42 billion light years, but supposedly the Universe is only 14 billion years old. How has the Universe expanded faster than the speed of light? Current science is always only our best guess, given what we perceive and our incredibly limited scope of understanding. Virtually everything we believe to be true...is not. For me, this means we can totally reinvent ourselves, and our personal Universes.

> **Rather than being your thoughts and emotions, be the awareness behind them.**
> **Eckhart Tolle**

Levels of Consciousness

There are many definitions and variations of consciousness. Eastern philosophy has Advaita Vedanta, Om Mantra, Veda, Zen, Buddhism and Ananda Sangha. Western versions are based more on the psychology of man—Freudian models, Holder's three levels of consciousness, Barrett's seven levels of personal consciousness, Gibson's four states of consciousness, etc. What they all agree on is a systematic migration from low vibrating, physical emotions and behavior to high vibrating emotions, spiritual awakening and ascendance.

Our emotions and our behavior are the signals we send out that indicate what level of consciousness we are currently experiencing. The vibration level of that consciousness level attracts thoughts and actions synonymous with its energy resonance. So, we have an obvious measure of where we each stand on this staircase to consciousness—we simply have to monitor and assess our emotions.

> **In its ultimate essence, energy may be incomprehensible by us except as an exhibition of the direct operation of that which we call Mind or Will.**
> **Sir Ambrose Fleming**

Power vs Force

Power vs Force is an interesting book written by David Hawkins. Through kinesiology, he tested thousands of people and measured the energy level of emotions, then set them out on a scale of low to high:

Shame: (vibrates at level 20)
Shame is obviously a negative emotion and incorporates both fear (of known/unknown) and self-loathing (temporary or permanent). It is destructive to emotional and psychological health and makes us prone to physical illness.

Guilt: (30)
Guilt manifests itself in a variety of expressions, such as remorse, self-recrimination, masochism, and victimhood. Unconscious Guilt results in psychosomatic disease, accident proneness and suicidal behavior.

Apathy: (50)
This level is characterized by depression, poverty, despair, and hopelessness. Apathy is a state of helplessness where the afflicted lack the resources and the energy to start a recovery process.

Grief: (75)
This is the level of sadness, loss and dependency. Those at this level live a life of constant regret and depression. This is the level of mourning, bereavement, and remorse about the past. Creation is easier to manifest at higher emotions. A depressed person cannot manifest – depression is low frequency and attracts low frequency manifestation.

Fear: (100)
Fear is all-consuming and may take any form. Fear limits growth of the

personality and leads to inhibition. Positive energy is required to shift out of this level, and often the person cannot make this shift on their own.

Desire: (125)
Desire is a need to fulfil neuro-chemical addictions. Where we fulfil the desire, we are temporarily satisfied. Where the desire is not fulfilled, we are left anxious, angry, or despondent. The need to change this often leads to impulsive and irresponsible actions. This can lead downwards if it leads to fear (of consequence) or guilt. But it can lead upward if anger is the outcome.

Anger: (150)
When we experience anger our primitive brain is in control of our thoughts, emotions and anger. Our primitive brain is low-vibrational and not a high form of consciousness. Anger can lead to violence, hate, regret and suppressed emotions. It can also be a shift up in one's emotional state, if they were previously in fear. The trick is not to get stuck in a state of anger.

Pride: (175)
Although a 'low' level because it vibrates at less than 200, pride is a positive level for somebody at lower levels. Pride is owned by the ego, and in consciousness terms the ego is only slightly higher than our primitive minds. In pride, reactive emotions abound such as hubris, arrogance, separation, false values, and feelings of superiority. The ego often senses being attacked, and this leads back to primitive emotions.

Courage: (200)
The 200 level is significant because this is the level where 'Force' is replaced by 'Power'. Courage takes us on a growth journey where we experience resourcefulness, achievement, fortitude, and determination. As David Hawkins writes in his book *Power vs Force*: "At the lower levels the world is seen as hopeless, sad, frightening, or frustrating, but at the level of Courage, life is seen to be exciting, challenging, and stimulating. At this level of empowerment, one is able to cope with and effectively handle the opportunities of life. Hence growth and education become attainable goals. Obstacles that defeat people whose consciousness is

below 200, act as stimulants to those who have evolved into the first level of true power. People at this level put back into the world as much energy as they take; at the lower levels, populations as well as individuals drain energy from society without reciprocating."

Neutrality: (250)
Energy becomes more positive at this level. Below 250, we see the duality of the world: up/down, black/white, us versus them. This leads to judgment and separation. Neutrality starts us on the path of non-judgmental behavior, less rigidity in our behavior, and less attachment to expected outcomes. There is a sense of safety at this level, because we no longer feel attacked when we do not get our own way, we no longer seek to control others and do not feel frustration when our desires are not met. People in this level seek to avoid conflict and see the futility of the various conflicts around the globe.

Willingness: (310)
People at this level are open minded and optimistic, display expertise and brilliance in their occupation or endeavor, display a high degree of inventiveness or intuition, and achieve social and economic success. They do not fear their inner issues and self-reflect in order to resolve the issue (for instance, they analyze their anger and see that it is a negative emotion and remove it from their behavior). They accept the balance in life and see adversity, persecution, injury, misery and oppression as the necessary balancing action of the good fortune they experience.

Acceptance: (350)
As already discussed, we individually create our existence and all our experiences. At the level of acceptance, this realization starts to dawn, and sparks an intensive self-search for the Truth, origin and destination of your soul. People at this level no longer see things as external and realize that the capacity for love and joy is within themselves, that they alone are responsible for the creation of their bliss. As David Hawkins wrote: "The individual at this level isn't interested in determining right or wrong, but instead is dedicated to resolving issues and finding out what to do about problems. Long-term goals take precedence over short-term ones; self-discipline and mastery are prominent."

Reason: (400)
Our emotions are generated and experienced by the lower levels of our consciousness. At the level of reason, we surmount our base emotions and develop a grasp of conceptualization and comprehension. No longer do desires such as lust and greed control us, instead we seek knowledge and education, to perform charitable acts, and altruism. People at this level display a social conscience, and magnanimous behavior. Whilst these people understand reason and truth, only some master that reason does not necessarily lead to Truth.

Love: (500)
In the next chapter I discuss the four levels of love: storge, philia, eros and agape. The first three are all human forms of love, low consciousness love deriving from fulfilment of our addiction to the neurochemicals dopamine, serotonin and oxytocin; the fourth, agape, is spiritual love. As David Hawkins writes: "The 500 level is characterized by the development of a Love that is unconditional, unchanging, and permanent. It doesn't fluctuate—its source isn't dependent on external factors. Loving is a state of being. It's a forgiving, nurturing, and supportive way of relating to the world. Love isn't intellectual and doesn't proceed from the mind; Love emanates from the heart. Love focuses on the goodness of life in all its expressions and augments that which is positive. This is the level of true happiness."

Joy: (540)
People at this level only experience unconditional love which induces a permanent feeling of joy. Each moment is bliss. They display unwavering belief and patience despite massive trials and tribulations. They are consumed by compassion for the world and everything in it. They see the world as a place of peace, beauty and happiness (because these are manifested from within). They are capable of manifesting high-level events, and even miracles.

Peace: (600)
Transcendence, self-realization, and God-consciousness are the main experiences at this level. As per David Hawkins': "Perception at the level of 600 and above is sometimes reported as occurring in slow motion,

suspended in time and space—nothing is stationary, and all is alive and radiant. Although this world is the same as the one seen by others, it has become continuously flowing, evolving in an exquisitely coordinated evolutionary dance in which significance and source are overwhelming. This awesome revelation takes place non-rationally, so that there is an infinite silence in the mind, which has stopped conceptualizing. That which is witnessing and that which is witnessed take on the same identity; the observer dissolves into the landscape and becomes, equally, the observed."

Enlightenment: (700–1,000)
A person at this level would not experience individual persona, nor the physical body. They are powerful manifestors and influencers. They vibrate at such a high level that they perceive the complete electromagnetic spectrum and are aware of the energy-based creation. They completely identify with The Divine, to the point that they are One with the Divine. This is the level of ascended masters.

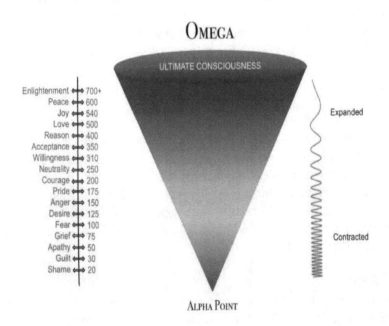

As depicted in this diagram, lower levels of emotion equate with lower levels of consciousness. Higher levels of emotion equate with higher levels of consciousness. The numbers allocated (for instance 600 for Peace) are logarithmic, and not a linear increase on the previous emotion. The measurement was obtained through kinesiological testing. The calibrations are not an arithmetic progression, but rather a logarithmic progression—so that 300 is not twice the level of 150, it is 300 to the tenth power (300^{10}). An increase of only a few points represents a major advance in power.

In essence, understanding that our emotional state is connected to our consciousness level offers a tool to increase your ability to create.

The Emotional Guidance Scale

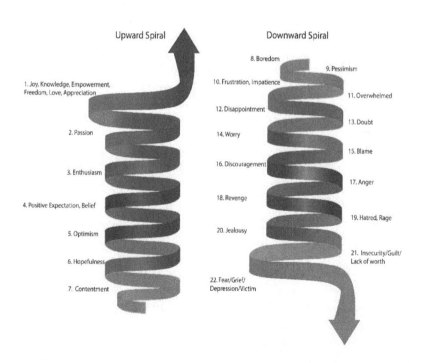

Using your emotions is a way to identify where on the emotional spiral you are, and to determine strategies to initiate an upward movement. The emotional guidance system was developed by Abraham Hicks and is a good graphical representation.

This scale is used as part of the "Emotional Guidance System" and "22 Processes" as outlined in the book *Ask and it is Given, Learning to Manifest Your Desires* by Esther and Jerry Hicks. They stress two main aspects: firstly take baby steps until you try to step up a level—immerse yourself in the level you are at, feel the full experience of it—before again moving upwards; secondly, ensure that you have dealt with emotions in the previous level completely.

Take the example of a person who recently lost their partner to death. They are in the Grief/Depression phase. If they were elevated to an Optimism level too soon, there would be many emotions they had needed to work through, that were "skipped." They cannot be healed until these emotions have been experienced and discarded.

> **Consciousness grows with age.**
> **Confucius**

Solipsism

Solipsism is a philosophical theory which asserts that nothing exists but the individual's consciousness. This has certain validity, as it is impossible to verify anything but our own consciousness.

Left Brain versus Right Brain Consciousness

Amazingly, whether we are left- or right-brained affects how we experience consciousness. A left-brain dominant person (generally) believes they are a separate entity, an individual not connected to any higher power. A right-brain dominant person (generally) believes in a sense of unity with a higher power, either religiously, spiritually or metaphysically. These opposing beliefs might explain the ongoing war of viewpoints between science, religion and spiritualists.

Learning to Pause

Our sympathetic system has a faster response time than our parasympathetic system. This is for one good reason—survival. Imagine, in our caveman days, coming face-to-face with a threat— let's say a saber-toothed tiger—our sympathetic system triggers our fight or flight response which floods the body with adrenalin.

The downside of this phenomenon is that our reactions are quicker than our reasoning. Have you ever instantly spoken or acted in retaliation to a person who made you angry and then either immediately, or later, regretted your action? Your reaction was an overreaction and, after having had time to think about it, and listen to your reasoning, you realized that the threat was insignificant, and/or your sympathetic system enlarged it and blew it out of proportion. We see this with dogs at any home: the doorbell rings and the hounds of hell let loose an awful cacophony of barking demons.

Part of our spiritual growth in our human experiment is to learn pause: to learn not to immediately react; to learn to consider something before responding. This Zen-like skill is a major steppingstone on our path to consciousness.

Chapter 8 – The Conscious, Subconscious and Unconscious

The Three (or Four) Minds

The conscious mind's function is to assimilate and interpret input from all five human senses. It then sends these interpretations to the subconscious mind for processing. The subconscious mind manages these inputs by controlling what they do to the body or by what action the person takes. On average, the subconscious determines our reaction one-third of a second before our conscious mind or body reacts. This differs between people—for instance, the reaction time for an athlete with "good" reactions (reflexes) is faster than most.

There is obviously no physical distinction between the conscious, subconscious and unconscious. If there is, it has not been proven or accepted. For our purposes we accept them as virtual minds. But research is being done in this field and, as human science progresses, important facts regarding these three entities might well be uncovered.

The conscious mind is what you are using right now to read these words. It is your awareness of who you are, where you are, whether you are hot or cold, hungry or not, etc. It is your ability to use logic, to make decisions and to analyze a puzzle, or to perform any voluntary muscle contraction.

The subconscious mind is like the hard drive on your computer, a storage area for memories, experiences, feelings, emotions, etc. But it also contains your "applications"—your beliefs, morals, values, motivators and de-motivators. Your subconscious mind never sleeps. During sleep, your lungs, heart, circulation, digestive system and other organs all continue functioning.

The unconscious mind is your primitive mind, containing your most basic programs that allow you to function and survive. These include breathing, heartbeat, digestion, and cellular metabolism. We cannot access the unconscious mind, and this is probably a survival mechanism—you cannot voluntarily stop breathing for long periods or stop your heartbeat. In terms of our computer analogy, this is your basic operating system.

Different brainwave states are associated with the different minds. The recent discovery of Epsilon (<0.5 Hz) and Lambda (>100 Hz) brainwave lengths lays the foundation of the basis for **the superconscious mind**.

Historically, a dubious claim was made that we only use 10% of our brains. The famous speaker Bruce Lipton (7 Ways to Reprogram Your Subconscious Mind) has another theory regarding 90/10: he states that 10% of our brain consists of neurons, and 90% consists of glia. Together they make up 100% of our brain. According to him we have access to 100% of our brain, but only tend to re-use the portions where we have developed "neural" pathways. Scientists analyzing Einstein's brain found a larger ratio of glial cells to neurons, as compared to a "normal brain."

They concluded that the greater number of glial cells per neuron indicates that the neurons had an increased metabolic need—they needed and used more energy, causing Einstein to have better thinking abilities and conceptual skills.

> **The unconscious mind operates at 40 million bits of data per second, whereas the conscious mind processes at only 40 bits per second.**
> **Bruce Lipton**

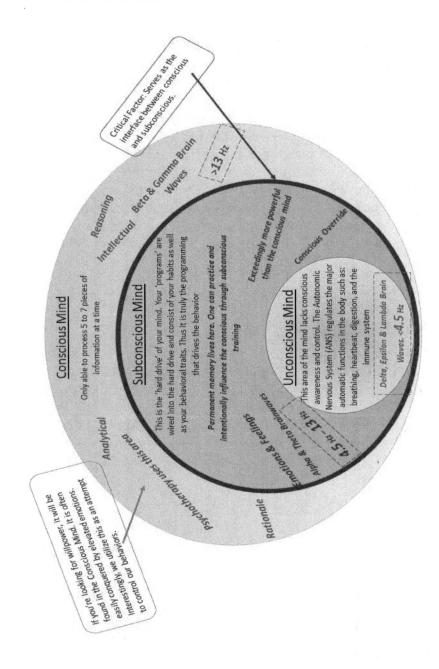

Critical Factor: Serves as the interface between conscious and subconscious.

>13 Hz

Conscious Mind

Reasoning

Intellectual   Beta & Gamma Brain Waves

Only able to process 5 to 7 pieces of information at a time

Subconscious Mind

This is the 'hard drive' of your mind. Your 'programs' are wired into the hard drive and consist of your habits as well as your behavioral traits. Thus it is truly the programming that drives the behavior

Permanent memory lives here. One can practice and intentionally influence the conscious through subconscious training

Exceedingly more powerful than the conscious mind

Conscious Override

Unconscious Mind

This area of the mind lacks conscious awareness and control. The Autonomic Nervous System (ANS) regulates the major automatic functions in the body such as: breathing, heartbeat, digestion, and the immune system

Delta, Epsilon & Lambda Brain Waves <4.5 Hz

Emotions & Feelings

Alpha & Theta Brainwaves

4.5 – 13 Hz

Rationale

Analytical

Psychotherapy uses this area

If you're looking for willpower, it will be found in the Conscious Mind. It is often easily conquered by elevated emotions. Interestingly, we utilize this as an attempt to control our behaviors.

What are the differences between the minds?
This question has led to much debate, and there is no clear winning argument. I like to think of the different minds in terms of the wavelength or vibrational frequency that they are operating at:

Mind	Wavelength	Hertz
Conscious mind	Mid Alpha to Beta	[10 Hz to 30 Hz]
Subconscious mind	High Alpha to Delta	[13 Hz to 4 Hz]
Unconscious mind	Delta	[4 Hz to 0.5 Hz]
Superconscious mind	Epsilon and Lambda	[< 0.5 Hz and >100 Hz]

For the purpose of this book, and in order not to enter into the various arguments of subconscious versus unconscious versus superconscious, from this point on I refer to them jointly as the subconscious.

The Kabbalah talks about "chochma" (expansive subconsciousness) and "binah" (the conscious mind). The Kabbalah also speaks of the fact that creativity is housed in the right brain and analytical thought in the left. Freud and Jung were familiar with these Kabbalistic works and this is apparent in some of their teachings.

The conscious and subconscious minds each have control over specific areas of our functioning:

Conscious Mind	Subconscious Mind
Responsible for logic and reasoning	Runs the body (autonomic function)
Responsible for math calculations	Stores and organizes all memories
Responsible for analysis	Governs emotions
Responsible for decision making	Works on the principle of least effort
Responsible for thinking	Chooses the path of least resistance
Seat of intellect	Represses memories with an unresolved emotion

Conscious Mind	Subconscious Mind
Responsible for details	Presents repressed memories for resolution
Responsible for organization and planning	Controls and maintains all perceptions
Seeks outcomes to meet desires	Seeks to return to homeostasis
Communication via language	Maintains instinct and habit
Awareness of self	Self-preservation is its highest ideal
Awareness of thought	Responds to symbols
Awareness of environmental conditions	Perception is reality
Interpreter of subconscious desire	Does not process negatives
Interprets physiological signals (e.g. pain)	Controls autonomic processes
Communicates through thought and language	Communicates through emotion and symbols
Slow learning process	Makes associations and learns quickly
Voluntary muscle action	Involuntary muscle action
Sleeps	Is always awake
Governs the five senses	Governs the sixth sense / intuition

The conscious mind is capable of learning literally or inferentially, depending on whether you are left or right brained. The subconscious mind can only learn literally.

The Pain and Pleasure Principle

All human behavior is motivated by two things—seeking pleasure and avoiding pain.

Freud identified the instinctive relationship between pain and pleasure. We seek pleasure and avoid pain in order to satisfy biological and psychological needs. In infancy and early childhood, our behavior is ruled by obeying only the pleasure principle. At that age we seek immediate gratification, aiming to satisfy cravings such as hunger and thirst, and at later ages the ego seeks out pleasure-filling activities such as sex and acquisition.

> **The secret of success is learning how to use pain and pleasure instead of having pain and pleasure use you. If you do that, you're in control of your life. If you don't, life controls you.**
> **Tony Robbins**

The reality principle describes the capacity to defer gratification. This is a consciousness jump, where we deny the insistence of the reptilian brain, and make a conscious decision to avoid pleasure seeking. This might be a temporary delay (delayed gratification) or a permanent delay (denied gratification).

The reason for the denial is most important. If it is for the purpose of self-improvement or spiritual growth, then this is positive. We call it self-control, and it is a sign of maturity and stability. However, if the denial is self-punishment, then this is negative. Self-punishment comes in two forms:

- I am not worthy. I do not deserve pleasure
- I must be punished—a masochistic self-denial in order to cause pain rather than pleasure

There is a belief that insists the subconscious mind "knows" what is best for you and uses the pain and pleasure principle to guide you to and away from experiences. This is a complex process when you consider that drug use, as an example, starts as a pleasure and becomes great pain when it leads to drug abuse.

The relationship between pain and pleasure could be considered a reward-punishment based system. Perceived pleasure is associated with reward; perceived pain with punishment. From an evolution standpoint this is highly functional as actions that lead to pleasure release chemicals that help reset our parasympathetic system and homeostasis - for example, we eat food because it releases pleasure sensations, and food is critical for our survival. The process is also valid for pain: pain teaches us to avoid specific events and situations; this leads us to develop a defense and survival strategy.

> **Nature has placed mankind under the governance of two sovereign masters, pain and pleasure.**
> **Jeremy Bentham**

Chemical Drivers – "DOSE"

Let's look at how the brain works so you understand how you can bring about change. If you were to take away consciousness, then a human being is a simple animal driven by reptilian urges. At our base level we are motivated to perform actions by an internal release of body chemicals, hormones and neurotransmitters into the mind and into the body.

"Positive" Chemicals	Mind Link
Dopamine	Is a feeling of success
Oxytocin	Is a feeling of trust
Serotonin	Is a feeling of self-esteem
Endorphins	Is a feeling of euphoria

Ever heard the acronym "DOSE"? It stands for dopamine, oxytocin, serotonin and endorphins. At our lowest level, our body is made up of chemical elements with some electricity. At a level slightly further up, we are simply reptilian animals, whose behavior is driven by the addiction to these four chemicals—and others such as acetylcholine and GABA. We are made up of chemicals and are programmed to seek out and fulfil a chemical "fix."

We associate with, and desire, the release of additional chemicals (like acetylcholine), but the above four are the main ones. Even human "love" is only a release of chemicals at its base level. Take oxytocin as an example—this "trust" chemical is released in various situations: suckling a breast (mother/child), sex (both partners), playing with a pet (pet/owner), hugs (both huggers), kissing (both kissers) and intimate touch (toucher/touched). The Greeks recognized four different kinds of love and they each induce varying levels of release of neurochemicals:

- *storge* is the natural affection parents have for their children, familial love
- *eros* is romantic love
- *philia* is love for a "thing"
- *agape* is unconditional love

Obviously, everything is subjective, based on whether you like it or you don't. But it is the chemical release that determines whether you like it or you don't. In effect, we are rewarding ourselves with chemicals that we make ourselves for activities/actions that we ourselves determine the value/priority of! This is all about you—nothing external has interfered with this process. In short, we can learn new behaviors and assign an appropriate chemical release to reinforce the value of this new behavior.

The feel-good chemicals are perceived as pleasure, and the feel-bad chemicals (like cortisol) are perceived as pain. Chemicals like acetylcholine lead to relaxation which stimulates our reward center and is thus perceived by our mind-body as "good." Chemicals like epinephrine and norepinephrine stimulate the sympathetic nervous system, lead to a heightened state—such as fight or flight, fear and anxiety—and are perceived by the reward center as "bad." An absence of feel-good chemicals does not feel right, and you are programmed to achieve the release of them. If we encounter opinions or facts that align with ours, dopamine is released; if we encounter opinions or facts that are in opposition to what we believe then norepinephrine is released. At a base level, this is nothing more than a teaching process, where our behavior becomes Pavlovian. The teachable lessons (our "path") are driven by the subconscious according to a predetermined set of rules. We seek out the "good" and avoid the "bad."

You are generally in an upward or downward emotional spiral. Hormones affect behavior, which affects the release of hormones. If we are in an upward spiral, positive hormones are released which creates positive behavior, which creates positive hormone release. This upward spiral will continue until an external event forces the release of negative hormones, which creates negative behavior, which then creates negative hormone release—a downward spiral.

Another concept to consider is balance. The neurohormones need to be released together, and in relative amounts. When too much dopamine is released too frequently, and without the balancing effect of simultaneous release of other hormones, our body becomes desensitized to dopamine. This means we build up a tolerance and need more dopamine more often to achieve the same "high." This leads to addictive behavior. A balanced simultaneous release of hormones ensures that receptors are "filled" concurrently with a combination of the various neurohormones, and not just dopamine. Too little or too much of any one neurochemical is problematic. People with Parkinson's disease have been linked to low levels of dopamine and people with schizophrenia have been linked to high levels of it. If we artificially try to increase one neurochemical, it usually comes at the expense of another—take selective serotonin reuptake inhibitors (SSRIs) for instance: a person will take an SSRI to increase serotonin, but SSRIs block the production of dopamine. Sadly, this is indicative of Western medicine; not only do they treat the symptom and not the cause, the 'medicine' typically has unwanted side effects.

Acetylcholine has a tranquilizing effect on the body and nervous system. It is released anytime the vagus nerve is stimulated; in this regard, deep breathing is an effective way to achieve stimulation and therefore acetylcholine release. The act of smoking involves taking deep inhalations; this releases acetylcholine with its tranquilizing effect on the person—this is the main reason smokers cannot quit, they become addicted to the relaxing effect of acetylcholine.

The dominant neurotransmitters for the left brain are dopamine and acetylcholine, and for the right brain norepinephrine. The different chemicals appeal to either side of our brains which evoke a certain behavioral response. Whether we are left- or right-brained determines much of our character and behavior. But our emotional state and external events both generate specific chemicals inside us that can affect which side of our brain is dominant at any given time. This also explains why we are not just left-brained, or just right-brained. We constantly cross over between the two.

The delivery of body chemicals, particularly endocrine and neurotransmitters, affect us greatly. Obtaining a balance in these chemicals is important. Take serotonin for instance: too much serotonin can cause high blood pressure, confusion, and even aggression, psychosis, and strokes. If it is too low, we get insomnia, anxiety, even violence and suicide. A deficiency of serotonin is connected to a range of disorders such as anorexia, aggression, alcoholism, anxiety, autism, depression, Down's syndrome, and seasonal affective disorder (SAD). The Law of Balance extends even to the neurochemicals inside us.

Pavlovian Humans

When we recognize that all our behavior, emotions and responses are conditioned by our need for these chemicals we can start to assess our consciousness. When we start to elevate our behavior, emotions and responses to align with our higher mind, we move from Pavlovian human to sentient being.

One dictionary describes sentient as:
- things that are alive, able to feel and perceive, and show awareness or responsiveness
- endowed with feeling and unstructured consciousness
- consciously perceiving

Our addiction to chemicals lends us to domination by our primitive mind. The more we engage in this behavior, the stronger our primitive mind becomes. At some stage we encounter a "consciousness shift"—a point where we realize that we are more than chemically addicted animals, and that there is a higher purpose for ourselves. When this happens, we have started on the path to consciousness.

Chapter 9 – Increase Your Resonance

According to Tracy this is the crux of the matter. What level are you vibrating at, where do you want to be vibrating, and what to do to bridge the gap? She already has a great understanding of what is discussed here, has been applying it for many years, and therefore skips all the science and goes straight to creation by assessing her vibrational level.

Recently she was having a difficult time, and when things couldn't seem to get any lower, she realized how her state of mind was affecting the rest of the family. This was the motivation she needed to make a change. Within two days she was a different person and the energy shift in the house was palpable.

She began editing this book and said it helped her get in touch with what she already knew and reminded her to get back to gratitude. For her, bridging the gap, means getting in touch with gratitude.

What is a Body Vibration Level?

In this book I have tried to keep metaphysics to a minimum and rather focus on the physical mechanics of the Law of Creation. The whole concept of Consciousness Engineering is detailed in this book because our behavior is linked to our mind-body and to effectively change we must understand that we are Consciousness Engineers.

According to Wikipedia https://en.wikipedia.org/wiki/Resonance, "In physics, resonance is a phenomenon that occurs when a vibrating system or external force drives another system to oscillate with greater amplitude at a specific preferential frequency. Frequencies at which the response amplitude is a relative maximum are known as ... resonant frequencies."

A famous Nikola Tesla quote is "If you want to find the secrets of the universe, think in terms of energy, frequency and vibration."

Everything in creation, both animate and inanimate, is made up of moving energy. At the atomic and sub-atomic level there is movement of energy—wherever there is movement of energy there is vibration, and vice versa. Vibration can be described as a periodic or cyclic motion between two extremes around a mid-point, a guitar string for example. When the string is plucked it moves in a cycle between two extremes around a mid-point, causing a sound wave to be produced at a particular note, or frequency.

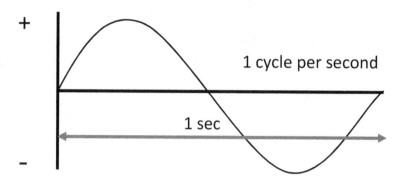

The frequency is how many times, or cycles, are repeated in one second, and is referred to as Cycles Per Second (Cps).

Everything that vibrates resonates at a fundamental or primary frequency, based on the configuration of energy that holds the matter together. So, in simple terms you—every part of you—your mind, and your environment, are all continually vibrating. Each element has a specific vibration, or range of vibration, when it is functioning "properly."

Take the human brain as an example. A typical healthy brain resonates between 72–90 Hz. When a brain's vibration drops below 72 Hz, it starts to become erratic, illness can form, memory becomes bad, delusions may occur, etc. Everything around us has vibration and impacts our vibration. For instance, the food we put in our bodies will maintain, increase, or decrease our vibration level. If we continually eat organic food, clean energized water, and breathe mountain air, then our vibration will remain high. Conversely, if we eat GMO food, drink sodas, consume sugar, and breathe Beijing-type smog then our vibration level will be negatively impacted.

Similarly, if we live a pure life, have religious or spiritual beliefs, are optimistic and positive, have a sense of humor, and have a purpose in life, then all of this helps maintain and raise our vibration level. Conversely, living a "dark" life (crime for instance), having no religious or spiritual beliefs, being negative and pessimistic with no sense of humor, leads to a lower vibration level.

Frequency of Various Things	
Human Brain	72-90 Hz
Human Body	62-68 Hz
Cold Symptoms	58 Hz
Flu Symptoms	57 Hz
Candida	55 Hz
Epstein-Barr Virus	52 Hz
Cancer	42 Hz
Onset of Death	25 Hz
Processed / Canned Food	0 Hz
Fresh Produce	Up to 15 Hz
Dry Herbs	12-22 Hz
Fresh Herbs	20-27 Hz
Essential Oils	52 – 320 Hz

The Chinese call this life energy Chi, or Qi, and the Buddhists call it Prana. It is the vibrational energy of our body.

The onset of death begins at 25 Hz. This low vibration is achieved by either one of the following two reasons: firstly, we have attracted lower vibrations, thus lowering our core vibration (such as bad habits, drug use, poor nutrition, etc.); OR, secondly, that we have lost our life energy and do not have the will to live (depression, old age, death of a spouse, etc.). A person might have a particular problem with one specific area of their body, for instance, their liver. The liver frequency is 55–60 Hz; when they are given homeopathic medicine, it engages to increase its vibrational range back into the normal range. The further away from the normal range the vibration drops, the more serious the disease. At the level of 58 Hz, diseases like cold and flu are more likely to appear. At lower levels (42 Hz) cancer starts to appear.

At lower frequencies we attract the similar lower vibrational entities such as disease, bacteria, virus and fungus. Disease and illness will not survive in an environment with a high vibrational energy. In the middle ages the black plague swept through Europe decimating the population. One group of people seemed resistant to the disease: the lavender girls who walked around with baskets of lavender selling to whoever would buy it. Lavender vibrates at 118 Hz, a very high vibration compared to our body and diseases. As a result of their daily interaction with this high vibration, their bodies were kept at a high vibration and this prevented them from succumbing to the plague. Nikola Tesla was right when he said that "If you could eliminate certain outside frequencies that interfered in our bodies, we would have greater resistance toward disease." Edgar Cayce said that "all strength, all healing of every nature is the changing of the vibrations from within, the attuning of the divine within the living tissue of a body to Creative Energies."

Crystals have a similar beneficial effect. Their high vibration helps maintain the body's range of vibrational energy and repels lower vibrational energies. Sound obviously has vibrational energy and of course it maintains, raises or lowers our vibration. A song we like appeals to the range of frequencies we are attracting or are attracted to. Classical music has a higher vibration than heavy metal. Gospel music has a higher vibration than rap. Also known as the "Aquarius Om," 432 Hz, is apparently the natural vibrational level of nature and is, therefore, deemed powerful.

When we consider that everything we connect with impacts us in a vibrational way (visually, orally, aurally, kinesthetically, sensually, intuitively) then we might wish to be discerning about what we eat, and what we listen to. A glass shatters when impacted by sound at its core vibration (e.g. an opera singer can shatter the glass with her voice). But it only shatters because it has imperfections—flaws in the glass that vibrate at a lower level lead to its shattering. The metaphor here suggests that if we keep vibrating at a higher level then we keep the flaws out of our body.

Our thoughts each have their own vibration. An optimistic or "high" thought—like love, gratitude, charity, compassion—obviously has a higher vibration than hate, lust, envy, greed, jealousy. Vibrate high, people!

Ever had a craving for something? It is a desire by your body for a vibrational "fix." Drugs and alcohol are an attempt to change one's vibration. Whilst they bring a temporary sense of vibrational change, the end effect is a lowered vibration. Any stimulant (coffee for example) has a similar effect—an initial perceived positive vibrational change, followed by a negative effect. Think of the downer after a drug high, the hangover after excessive alcohol, and the flat period after a caffeine spike. Everything in our universe is in balance—you cannot have the high without the low. There is one exception to this—vibrational consciousness. If you were able to maintain an absolute aura of love and gratitude, for instance, there would not necessarily be a corresponding low. So, keep getting high on your thoughts as there is no negative effect.

How we live our life, and our homeostasis, affects our vibration level. For instance, ascetism is a lifestyle of Spartan-like deprivation, and is not beneficial as this behavior vibrates at a lower level; depriving oneself is a fear of something (e.g. we diet because of a fear of being rejected, we deprive ourselves for fear of getting fat). Balance is a good choice—as Ralph Waldo Emerson said: "Everything in moderation, especially moderation!" Each of us has a natural appetency, a requirement to fulfil the wants of a living organism. We should pursue this but be conscious of the ramifications of our choices. And as we make a "bad" choice, follow the philosophy of "there are no mistakes, only feedback." Accept the lesson, reprogram your mind, and make better choices. Let go of guilt, regret and shame—these are low vibrational energies!

Color has a vibrational energy, which is why you might prefer one color over another. Shapes have a vibrational energy—vegetable seedlings under a pyramid-type roof grow more quickly and with higher yield. Pyramids are very powerful vibration containers.

As mentioned earlier, Dr. Masaru Emoto's experiments with water crystals clearly prove the effect our thoughts, our words, our energy and our intentions have on water. Remembering that we are over 70% water, clearly your vibration level has a physiological impact on you, which in turn influences your vibration level.

In terms of vibrational energy, you can choose to be in an upward spiral, or a downward spiral. The important thing to understand is that you have the power over which direction you are going.

> **What we have called matter is energy, whose vibration has been so lowered as to be perceptible to the senses. There is no matter.**
> **Albert Einstein**

Sports professionals talk about being "in the zone"— that point of extreme focus where ability, skill, muscle memory and determination come together in such a way that they outperform their rivals. In effect, this is simply the athlete vibrating at such a high level that he or she attracts the success (attracts that probability from the Field of Probabilities).

There is a theory that you connect with your partner because they emit the frequency that you are looking for! And then you drift apart because they no longer emit that frequency, or you now need a different frequency. This concept is validated when you consider that emotions are the main reason we connect with a partner, and all emotions have different frequencies.

The Link Between Consciousness and Vibration

There is a direct link between consciousness and vibration. Our consciousness increases when our vibration increases, and vice versa.

> **We are not human beings on a spiritual journey, we are spiritual beings on a human journey.**
> **Stephen Covey**

Imagine that everything is on a spectrum. The range of light is infinite, as is the range of sound. The range of smells is probably also infinite, but to comprehend this is beyond the scope of our limited human senses. Light and sound are nothing more than energy vibrating at a particular frequency, and both are properties of the electromagnetic spectrum. Our ability as humans to discern and comprehend is so limited that it is narrowed down to a fraction of the "known" spectrum. I say known because frequency, like numbers, is infinite.

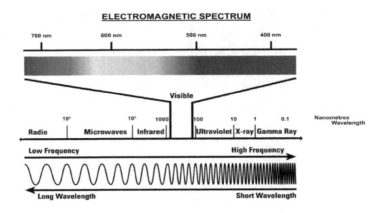

Visually, we can only see the spectrum covering dark red to violet. This is the visible color spectrum. We cannot see infra-red, or ultra-violet (yet some animals can). By obvious definition, we cannot see colors on the non-visible spectrum. We can only see one ten-trillionth of the electromagnetic spectrum! This underlines the fact that the spectrum of information that a human can discern is extremely limited.

On the one hand colors exist that we cannot see, and on the other we see colors that do not exist! Have a look at the spectrum. You will not see light pink, for instance. Because of the way the cones in our eyes work, they "perceive" pink even though it does not exist. Brown is another example, and there are many more. White light is a mixture of the colors of the visible spectrum. Black is a total absence of light. White light does not have its own electromagnetic wavelength level—it exists because we perceive that our eyes receive equal measures of all the wavelengths at the same time. Therefore, white light is a human creation, it does not exist in the universe we understand. You create white light! Now tell me you do not have the power to create...

To further push the boundaries of the incredulous: a banana is not yellow. An object receiving light absorbs all wavelengths of light, except the one it rejects (reflects). The object reflects this color. As it has absorbed all the other colors, technically it should be associated with those colors. Because we are simple humans, we act on what we think we see; we see the banana reflect the color yellow, so we consider the banana to be yellow. To again state the obvious, technically it is every color *except* yellow.

So, as humans we cannot perceive or understand most things that exist in the universe, and on the other hand we create things that supposedly do not exist! Part of consciousness is contemplating this juxtaposition. What we believe as individuals is not true, and consciousness is simply the search for truth.

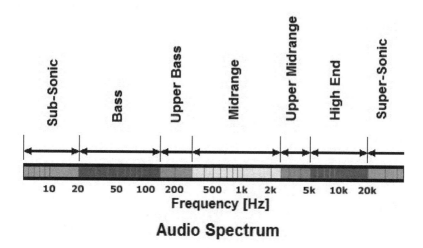

Audio Spectrum

Our hearing is similarly limited. The range that a human ear can interpret is usually cited as 20–20,000 Hz. Sound is infinite and continues below and above the limits of this spectrum. We cannot discern any sound that is sub-sonic or lower, nor super-sonic and higher. They are there but we are not equipped to "tune-in" to those sounds.

As frequency increases, the wavelength decreases, and energy increases. A Gamma wave, for instance has intense energy, high frequency and short wavelength. As our consciousness increases, so does our vibration, and our ability to perceive and understand vibrational things that were outside of our spectrum. Whenever electromagnetic waves exist in a medium with matter, their wavelength is increased. As humans, we are electromagnetically "dense", and our energy is slowed so that we assume physical qualities. The density of an object dictates how fast that energy can physically vibrate. Your subconscious is not dense and vibrates at a high level.

The things that we can sense are things whose vibration is reduced to a point on the spectrum that we can comprehend. All physical manifestations vibrate within certain ranges of frequency for human sense perception, like the visible color spectrum. People cannot perceive higher vibrational concepts because the frequency rate of vibration is outside the range of human perception, outside the "human understanding spectrum."

From this we can discern several solid facts:

1. Our senses are limited
2. What we see is not all there is
3. The universe is pure energy, vibrating
4. We cannot see or sense the majority of this energy, but we know it is there
5. A "thing" must vibrate at a relatively low level, and in a narrow band, for our senses to comprehend it. We cannot see, sense or tune-in to most of the aspects of the universe
6. We tend to deny, or resist, the stuff we cannot see, sense or tune-in to. This does not mean it is not there. On the contrary, the above evidence clearly shows it is there. So, we deny the majority of what is, and assume our small perceived knowns are fact, and the complete truth

A photon is an elementary particle, the quantum of light and all other forms of electromagnetic radiation. A photon is a discrete bundle (or quantum) of electromagnetic energy. When photons encounter the atoms of an object, the atom decides whether the photon will move the atom from one energy state to another and acts accordingly. It can re-emit the photon (scattering) which is what happens in the case of our banana; or it assimilates the photon (absorption); or the atom permits the passage of the photon with no action (transmission).

The first lesson we can pull from this is: As a simple human you experience this basic force of physics every day. Every day you encounter people (a compilation of photons vibrating at a low level), and events (which all have a vibration level). During your day you will have thoughts and feelings (both vibrating at a specific level). When these people, events, thoughts and feelings occur you have the power to choose whether to absorb, scatter or transmit the experience.

The second lesson is: what we perceive to be the absolute truth, is not. And there is so much "out there" that we cannot comprehend because of our low level of human vibration/consciousness. This is the basis for Plato's "The Allegory of the Cave" in his best-known work, The Republic. When I visited his cave, I could understand the concept that when we increase our vibration, our consciousness allows us to attract and comprehend a higher level of information. We can choose to reject this information and our vibration/consciousness will plateau and remain at the level we are comfortable with. Perhaps in our next life we will push ourselves to a higher level of vibration/consciousness.

Simply put, at a human level nothing that happens to us is real. We create its reality by how we choose to react. We are responsible for what we create. At a spiritual level, when our sense of individuality gives way to our universality, quantum shifts will be achieved in our vibration/consciousness.

*Wikipedia states "The limit for long wavelengths is the size of the universe itself, while it is thought that the short wavelength limit is in the vicinity of the Planck length. Until the middle of the 20th century it was believed by most physicists that this spectrum was infinite and continuous."

> **Man prefers to believe what he prefers to be true.**
> **Francis Bacon**

The Superconscious Mind – Epsilon Brainwave State

The electric cycle of your brain is known as the brainwave state. Typically, as you read this you are in a low Beta state, awake but relaxed. Recently, Epsilon and Lambda brainwave states were "discovered"—they were always there of course, but only recently were they actually measured in the brain. Epsilon is a brainwave state cycling at less than 0.5 Hz (extremely low frequency and high amplitude), and Lambda is a brainwave state cycling at more than 100 Hz (extremely high frequency and low amplitude).

> **In meditation, you must go beyond thought. As long as you are busy thinking, you are in your rational mind, on the conscious plane. When you sleep and dream, you are on the subconscious plane, and in your astral body. And when your mind is fully withdrawn on superconsciousness... That is the level of the soul's existence.**
> **Paramahansa Yogananda**

Many sources believe that Gamma is the harmonizing frequency—for example when you are observing an object its size, color, etc. are all perceived and processed by different parts of the brain, it is thought that Gamma allows for unification of all the different information. Theta and Gamma rhythms also interact helping the brain to package information into coherent images, thought and memories.

Extremely high brainwave frequencies above Gamma, 100 Hz and greater, have been identified by EEG researchers. These high-range brain frequency states are named Hyper-Gamma, and Lambda.

Totally opposite speed brainwave frequencies—some at 100 Hz and others at less than 0.5 Hz—have exactly the same states of consciousness associated with them. These Hyper-Gamma, Lambda and Epsilon frequencies, are linked together in a circular relationship. This brainwave activity is associated with states of self-awareness, higher levels of insight and information, psychic abilities and out of body experiences. This new region of brain activity and states of consciousness associated with it is called Epsilon.

The following diagram shows how Epsilon and Lambda brainwaves are conjoined, in that the frequencies mimic each other. Both states allow the subject to enter into a "Superconscious Mind" state.

Brain Wave States and Consciousness

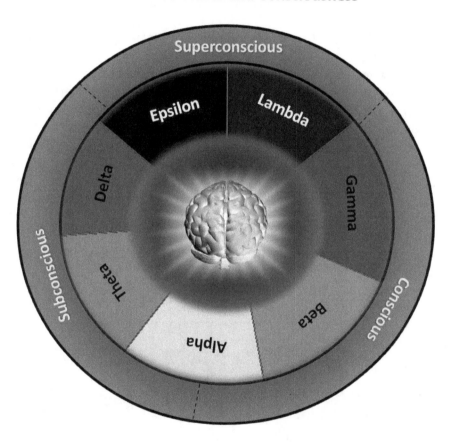

This Epsilon state of consciousness can be seen in patients where Western medical doctors perceive no heartbeat, respiration or pulse, but the person is still alive. Hyper-Gamma and Delta states of consciousness are the states Eastern mystics achieve in deep meditative practice.

Alpha is the beginning of the soul level, where we create our existence, and Epsilon/Lambda the deep soul state; the "God" state. Beta/Gamma is the ego level, where we exist and connect to the material, slow-vibrating world. The higher the brainwave state, the slower the material state. The lower the brainwave state, the faster the vibration in the material state. So, a higher vibration at one end leads to a lower vibration at the other end—this is simply the Law of Balance in action. The Law of Balance is one of the physical universe's most powerful laws.

Jesus, Buddha, and all the ascended masters realized that our Beta/Gamma state allows us to be present in the Earth experience. They were able to reach such a slow brainwave state that they were able to transcend this physical manifestation and were no longer material or physical. They were able to connect with their superconscious. According to Buddhism, a human being is born with 108 Earthly desires (such as attachment, jealousy and vanity). When we have Earthly desires, we vibrate at a low level in order to remain attached to this Earth. We are attached because of our attachment. Over time, and many lives, we realize the futility of Earthly desire and wish to manifest something else—this ultimately leads to Ascendancy.

A deep Alpha state—towards Epsilon/Lambda state—allows transfer of our consciousness deeper into the soul state. People experiencing a near-death experience enter a very low brainwave state (Delta/Epsilon) and can temporarily separate from their bodies. Then their brainwave state increases back up to Delta, and they return to their bodies.

> **That which can be seen has no form. That which has form cannot be seen.**
> **Buddhist Saying**

Vibration Level of Emotions

As discussed earlier, an emotion has a specific vibrational level. As you can imagine, joy + happiness + humor all vibrate at a high level, and depression + sadness + shame + guilt at a low level.

Similar to the electromagnetic spectrum, an emotional vibration spectrum is a continuum moving from low to high vibrational levels. The Abraham Hicks spiral (discussed earlier) shows the emotions that are linked to a positive upward spiral, and those linked to a negative downward spiral.

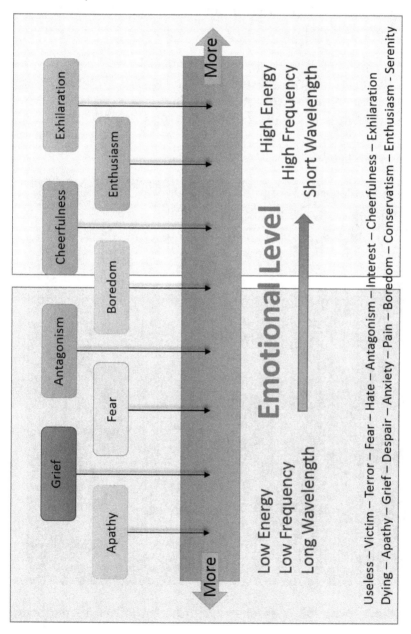

Each emotion has a specific vibrational level. Our emotion affects our behavior and vice versa. Behavior, emotions and consciousness are inextricably linked. You have to understand one to understand the mechanics of the others.

Upward emotions will increase our vibrational level, behaviors will improve, and this leads to a temporary increase in consciousness. Downward emotions will decrease our vibrational level, behaviors will worsen, leading to a temporary decrease in consciousness.

Raising Your Vibration Level

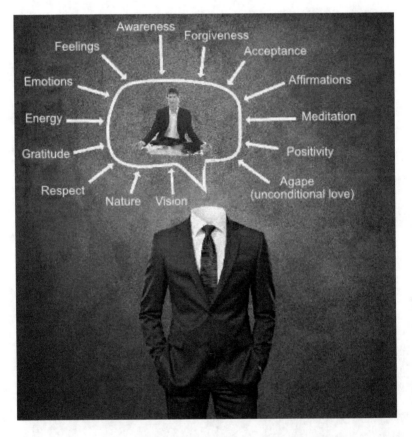

Nutrition – Nutrition is an energy source that influences the body's vibration. Taking in low-vibrational food will decrease your overall vibrational frequency, while high-vibrational food will increase it. This includes the intake of high-quality water, versus tap water and liquids containing alcohol or sugar versus freshly extracted vegetable juice for example. I won't go too heavily into nutrition here as this is not a book about food, but I discovered that animal flesh (meat, chicken, fish) all has a negative vibration. I was sure this was only according to vegetarians or vegans but could not find anything to refute it. I am a meat eater and therefore, before every meal, I bless my food. I give gratitude to the animals, the farmers, the logistics of getting it onto my plate and to the chef. By doing this, I believe I raise the vibrational energy of the food I am eating. Having said that, fresh, home cooked food is always vibrationally higher than fast, junk food and it tastes better!

Positive Thoughts and Optimism – What you think subconsciously is what you become. Positive thoughts vibrate at a higher level than negative thoughts. Your mind is a transmitter of signals and a receiver of equal signals. What you send out is what you will receive back. So, when you find yourself thinking thoughts that do not benefit you, have on call a memory that instantly uplifts your feelings. Focus on that to begin raising your vibration and to avoid being caught up in unwanted thoughts. Use your emotions as a guide to what your subconscious is thinking. Your emotions are a great signal to what is being triggered in your subconscious affording you the opportunity to rework them.

Emotions and Feelings – If thoughts are how the mind speaks to you, then emotions and feelings are how the body and the subconscious speaks to you. Feelings and emotions such as guilt and shame vibrate at a low level. Rid your life of these low-vibrational aspects, through meditation, or affirmations, or accessing a memory that invokes gratitude and love. Humor, love and joy all vibrate at a very high level. Love and gratitude combined have the highest vibrations.

Acceptance – Things will come, and things will go. Everything happens for a reason. Your resistance to anything is a signal you have not accepted it. For as long as you resist it, you will use valuable resources fighting it, and lower yourself into emotions of sadness, angst, anger, anxiety and stress.

These are all low-vibrating emotions. Accepting means courage and hope, and these are higher-vibrating emotions.

Forgiveness – The main lesson we each have in our lives is forgiveness. Forgiveness is the hardest thing in the world to master. But if achieved, leads to the most powerful gift—the gift of freedom. When we learn all that matters is our reaction to an event, we realize our own power. It leads to a realization that we create our own lives. It frees us of low-vibrational emotions such as revenge and anger and allows high-vibrational emotions such as love and acceptance. If you want to take forgiveness to the next level, the realization that there is nothing to forgive in the first place is immensely powerful.

Affirmations – When we affirm, we train our subconscious to believe a reality. When our subconscious believes something, it creates that reality. The body vibrates at a low level in order to manifest its physicality. The subconscious is not constrained by this physicality and vibrates at an extremely high level. Creation occurs at a high vibrational level.

Awareness/mindfulness – When we live in the past, we experience regret and nostalgia. When we live in the future, we experience anxiety and fear. Right here, right now, stop . . . and experience the most amazing thing: life. Something powerful created you, and for a powerful reason. Embrace the wonder of you and the life that represents.

Gratitude – As already stated, gratitude speeds up the creational process. We all wish to have a pleasant fulfilling life. Attachment to outcomes brings disappointment and anxiety. Stop the desiring for material things, and for things to be different. Instead, count all your blessings. And then give heartfelt thanks to the Universe (or God, god, the subconscious mind, your spirit guide, or WHOEVER!) for each and everything in your life. There is always something good in everything. Find the good and give gratitude for it. For example, you are sick in bed with the flu. What is there to be grateful for about that, after all you feel like you are dying? It could be that you desperately needed a rest and now your body has insisted you have one. It could be that your immune system is so strong that you are better in less than a week. Already, there are two good things in something bad that you can be grateful for – a well-deserved rest and a smashing immune system. The Universe gives you more of what you are grateful for—probably because you are telling the subconscious this is what you like; and the more you do it the more the subconscious is programmed. And the subconscious is a powerful creator. I would like to highlight that Gratitude does not make the 'bad' disappear from your life or this world, but there is always a bright side to everything, and The Law of Creation is all about what you focus on. Therefore, focusing on the good, will always bring about more good for you to focus on.

Meditation – We are not sure who we are, where we came from, or where we are going to. This is the root of consciousness, to determine Truth. We are not our body, or our brain, and we are not necessarily our mind either. We suffer from constant "noise," monkey chatter in our brains that confuses us, and prevents us from thinking clearly. Meditation removes the noise and allows us a clear channel to connect with our subconscious mind. In that connection we associate with our Source. Our Source improves our vibration level and our consciousness. Self-hypnosis is an additional tool that increases consciousness because of the similar aspects to meditation.

Agape (unconditional love) – We are all one. Like forgiveness, when this realization dawns it is a powerful gift. Why would you harm your neighbor when you are only harming yourself? We are all Part of the Whole. Agape is when you have unconditional love for the world and everybody in it; the same way you love your kids, for instance.

Selfless Giving – It is a force of nature that, whatever you give, you receive back many fold. When you give, you shout to the Universe that you are not fearful of lack, and that you are confident you have abundance. These are powerful and high vibrational statements. In addition, they state to your subconscious that you do not believe in lack, and you do believe in abundance. Your subconscious dutifully follows your beliefs by making this your reality. Research shows the body acts differently and positively to an individual's selfless giving, or acts with a noble purpose (eudaimonia) than to one's pleasurable experiences (hedonism). One is focused on self-gratification, and thereby attaches us to the Earth. The other is focused on other people or has a higher purpose, and therefore vibrates at a higher level. Eudaimonia literally means "good spirit." It is not necessary to give money, if you have it to give, then great. Acts of service are very high vibrational.

Positive Vision – We know how powerful guided imagery is. The athlete who wins the race, first won it multiple times in his, or her imagination. We know how powerful a vision board can be. The subconscious works with pictures, images and symbols. A vision board is a program you feed to your subconscious. It absorbs this program and starts to create the reality. This is the Law of Association in effect. The more you repeat the positive visions, the more effectively your subconscious is programmed. This is the Law of Repetition in effect. Positive visions create a higher vibrational existence.

Nature/elements – Nature vibrates at a high level. We refer to it as *prana* or *chi*, but it is vibrational energy. When we are in nature, we "soak up" this vibrational energy. This is one of the reasons super-foods are those that receive the most sunlight. In the same vein, sunlight is incredibly good for us, evident in the importance of the vitamin D we create in our bodies through sunlight. Nature/elements include the environment around us, which includes many items ranging from people we know, to our home and the music we listen to. This also includes the power of sound frequencies; music is a powerful consciousness changer. Chants such as "OMM" increase consciousness levels as this sound resonates at the earth's frequency of 7.83 Hz.

Chapter 10 – Cosmic Intelligence

To say we do not understand the Universe is an understatement. There are powerful, all-pervading forces we cannot explain, like quantum mechanics, magnetism, and gravity. Everything we see comprises more space than substance. Without the spaces, the Earth could be compressed into something

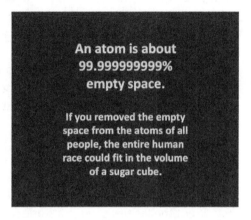

the size and shape of a rugby ball. And recently, plankton was found living on the outside of the International Space Station!

There is a groundswell of acceptance of new ideas, based on the current consciousness level. In the Middle Ages, it was accepted that the Earth was flat—because this fitted in with the known science of the day. We take today's known science as proof of our current beliefs. That science will change, and so will our beliefs.

Because of this, it is always a good idea to keep an open mind, open to all possibilities and opportunity.

I once read a book by William Hewitt, *Hypnosis for Beginners*. In it, Hewitt explains how he often enters into self-hypnosis, and then invites key historical figures into his life—entities such as Gandhi, Jesus, and Buddha. This resonated with me at once, and I copied him. I went into self-hypnosis, and invited people into my space. Strangely enough, the first person to come into my head was Nikola Tesla, whom I have always admired. The following day I was stunned when I realized I somehow knew "stuff"—stuff I had not read or seen on a TV show.

I was awed by how "easy" it is to connect to the source of intelligence and knowledge. Soon I had conversations with Jesus, Buddha, and

Einstein. Again, each day following my conversations, I had acquired new information. If this resonates with you, I recommend you try it:

1. Decide who you wish to converse with. Decide if this will be a "general" meeting, or if you have a specific issue you would like resolved.
2. Do self-hypnosis or deep meditation.
3. Vibrate at the energy of the person you wish to converse with. Thinking of that person, their works, their acts, their pictures, or their deeds, can help attain this level. Feel that vibration and attune to it.
4. Have a threshold event; mine was going down a staircase I used to own, into a wine cellar (don't ask!), and the person or people whom I invited would be sitting there.
5. Greet the visitor, offer gratitude for them and/or their deeds.
6. Ask either specific questions, or just "mind-meld"—have non-verbal communication. In some cases, the visitor spoke to me, but in most cases it was non-verbal.
7. Thank them for their time and go to sleep (if you are in bed) or wake yourself out of self-hypnosis.

There is a term for when someone suddenly gains access to information that is outside their knowledge: it is called hyper communication. Whatever you call it, and however you might connect to it, there is no doubt we are able to link to a collective consciousness. Hyper communication occurs naturally and often; ants, bees, and trees all use hyper communication to alert the proximity of food, or predators.

The Power of Prayer

What happens when people pray? In essence, they are vibrating at a higher frequency, the frequency of the Divine, the Universe, God, or call it what you will. Prayers are often "answered"—because vibrating at a certain frequency attracts similar vibrational energy. Praying typically attracts "good" events into your space.

Channeling

Channeling works on the same basis as the techniques outlined above. The channeler vibrates at the energy of the visitor and attracts that energy into their space.

As mentioned above, we have no idea how most of physics functions and behaves. Some possible theories for why the above techniques work are:

- **Akashic records** – supposedly a term coined by Rudolf Steiner, the Akashic records (based on the Sanskrit word for "sky," "space," "luminous," or "ether") are a compendium of all the thoughts, events, and emotions that have occurred in time, believed by theosophists to be encoded in a non-physical plane of existence known as the astral plane. This is also called the **Collective Consciousness.**
- **Cosmic intelligence** – as per the technique I used above, everything in life is energy and we merely have to vibrate at a specific vibrational level to attract the same vibrational energy. This manifests itself in thoughts, ideas, creations and inventions. Each of these items has its own vibration level.
- **Gene memory** – there is a theory that all of our life's experiences, from all of our ancestors, including reincarnations, are present in our DNA. In this regard we might "know" stuff which ordinarily we have not been exposed to. This is a collective consciousness.
- **Holographic Universe** – there is a theory, which is becoming stronger due to scientific research done that each one of our cells contains the complete program of the universe. In which case the knowledge is inside us and we merely have to connect to it.

Stories abound about people receiving information through their dreams, in the shower, or even a bump on the head! Dmitri Mendeleev, famous for compiling the Periodic Table of Elements, said that all the information came to him in a dream. Einstein woke up with a concept in his head, which then took him years to prove mathematically. August Kekulé was the father of organic chemistry, the concept of which appeared to him in a dream. Elias Howe had a problem with the first automatic sewing machine until a dream told him to put a hole in the tip.

Many people get "inspirational ideas" when they are in the shower, for instance. The shower, and act of showering, vibrate at a specific level that attracts inspiration. Other people might find inspiration in nature or looking at the stars at night. It's the same thing—it causes a vibration level that attracts thoughts and ideas.

Our subconscious is the most powerful creational tool in our universe. This is part of the Cosmic Intelligence—our subconscious mind is linked to everything. Our conscious mind gets in the way, and we insist on making choices based on ego and our skewed picture of our world. If we send the conscious mind into the background for a while, and allow our subconscious to take control, then amazing things start to happen. This is how hypnosis, meditation, affirmations etc. all work — we bypass our conscious mind and talk to the subconscious. From here on, let your subconscious mind do the heavy lifting!

When we drift off to sleep with any issue in our mind, we tend to wake up with a solution. This is because we moved into our subconscious for a period of time, and the subconscious is a puzzle solver. It produces a workable solution with very little effort. Meditation achieves the same state of bypassing our conscious and allowing our subconscious to step forward for a while and rectify our life.

Be aware of the concept of Cosmic Intelligence, and of the relationship between it and your subconscious mind. The Bible talks about "Ask and you shall receive." This is what cosmic Intelligence and your subconscious mind are all about.

Chapter 11 – Neuroplasticity: Habit, Neural Pathways and Neurogenesis

The word neuroplasticity is derived from the words 'neuron', meaning the nerve cells in our brain, and 'plastic'. Each individual neural cell is made up of an axon and dendrites and is linked to other cells by small spaces called synapses. The word plastic means to mold, sculpt, or modify. Neuroplasticity is the ability the brain has to recreate itself and regenerate itself, through the constant manufacture of new neural pathways.

For a long time, it was believed that brain cells could not regenerate, and we now know that this is not true. They regenerate regularly. In the same fashion we are capable of generating new neural pathways.

Every thought, movement, or experience is transformed into electro-chemical energy which is then stored in the brain. Our brain creates pathways that allow the energy to travel in a similar fashion each time the stimulation is triggered. The more it is triggered, the more common it becomes for it to travel that route. These are called Neural Pathways, and this is how habits are formed.

> **Your beliefs become your thoughts, your thoughts become your words, your words become your actions, your actions become your habits, your habits become your values, and your values become your destiny.**
> **Mahatma Gandhi**

Energy always takes the path of least resistance. If the habit happens to be a "bad" one (smoking for instance), and keeps getting reinforced, then it will become increasingly difficult to redirect the energy to a positive result. Every time we face the situation, the energy will take the same well-traveled path. To overcome this, we need to create a new path that will lead to a positive outcome. As we direct the energy towards a new path, the old path gets weaker. By rehearsing this new behavior in the hypnotic/imagery/NLP (Neuro-Linguistic Programming) state, we tread a new path.

Our brain is capable of growing new cells, making new connections, new neural pathways and generally re-developing itself. It may be difficult to start changing those neural pathways, but if we set our intention, and are mindful of the outcome, we will achieve it. If we spend only five minutes a day thinking about it, and perhaps doing affirmations, we will bring it about slowly. The more intense the energy, attention and focus, the sooner the results will be achieved. When we learn a new skill – like learning chess, or a new language, this creates new neural pathways.

Think of a determined person. That person will probably achieve their goal. Neuroplasty is the same—by continually submitting our mind to an idea or concept, the mind eventually accepts it. I do not know whether this is boredom (the mind eventually 'gives in'), or neuroplasty (the idea has traveled so many times in the brain it has developed a neural pathway) or repetition (like the media, when we are exposed to a concept we eventually start to believe it). Probably it is a combination of these factors. The important thing to know is that you have the ability to morph your brain (and yourself!) into a positive machine, a neurogenesis of sorts.

Affirmations work in the same way. By continually exposing our mind to an idea, or set of ideas, we change the plasticity of our brains. This is "neurobics"—in the same way that aerobic training is good for our body, neurobic training is good for our mind.

> **The greatest breakthrough in my lifetime is the realization that man can alter his life by altering his thinking.**
> **William James**

As detailed in his 1949 book *The Organization of Behavior,* Donald Hebb's work gave rise to the notion that "neurons that fire together, wire together." When neuron A "fires" neuron B, the link between the two grows stronger. Any experience, thought, feeling, and physical sensation "fires" thousands of neurons, which form a neural network. When we repeat an experience over and over, the brain learns to fire the same neurons each time. This ends up as what we call a habit. Muscle memory works along similar lines. Repetition of action and thought leads to mastery of a particular process.

Hebb's Law is the journey that takes us from Unconscious Incompetence (I do not know what I cannot do), to Conscious Incompetence (I know what I cannot do), to Conscious Competence (I have learned to do it) to Unconscious Competence (I can do it without thinking about it). Learning to drive is a good example of this.

His work also led to the entity of the "engram"—the method of storing memories as biochemical entries in the brain. Although a memory is distributed among various neural systems, specific types of knowledge may be processed and contained in specific regions of the brain (like the occipital lobe being responsible for vision processing). By continually using our brain, and exercising it through thought process and puzzle solving, we create neural pathways that keep the brain functioning and healthy and increase the density of the grey matter.

Consider the analogy of a journey through a dense forest. Initially it is tough going. Second time around it is a little easier. After twenty-one journeys we have started to develop a well-worn path. This is a neural pathway. Now consider stepping off the well-worn path into the dense jungle again—this taxes our systems and we tend to avoid it. Assume we followed the new path and stuck to it for a period of time, then the initial path would start to get overgrown. Our new habits replace our old in this fashion.

Another way of looking at this is when we have a new thought we have created a dirt path in our mind; then we create words which widen this path; these words lead to actions which widen the path; these actions lead to experiences which create a freeway; the actions and experiences create a habit, which is a super-highway in your mind.

Chapter 12 – Neuro-Linguistic Programming (NLP)

In simple terms, "neuro-linguistic" refers to the way our minds process language, and "programming" to our ability to process that which we perceive through our five senses.

Somebody once said you cannot succeed unless, in your mind, you have become the one who already succeeded. Simply put, if the subconscious mind believes it, then it is real. NLP is an effective modality for reprogramming our subconscious minds, and in improving our behavior in general. In short, NLP is how to use the language of the mind to consistently achieve our specific and desired outcomes.

In its simplest form, NLP is the concept that the way we think, and the words we use, are a reflection of who we are, and how we see the world. We know that what we think is what we become. If we have a complaint/issue/illness, then we created it through our model of the world (how we see things). So, it stands to reason that we need to un-create our model and recreate something better. We need to rethink our words, thoughts, attitudes and actions.

What Does Neuro-Linguistic Programming Mean

Let's look at the words "Neuro," "Linguistic" and "Programming"—at first it seems like a complicated title.

Neuro obviously refers to the brain and the neural processes. Neurons are the messengers used by the nervous system to send, receive, and store signals we receive.

These external signals are derived from the five senses, known by the acronym **VAKOG**:

- Visual (messages we see)
- Auditory (messages we hear)
- Kinesthetic (sensation of touching and being touched)
- Olfactory (messages we smell)
- Gustatory (messages we taste)

In addition, we generate internal signals such as thoughts, feelings and emotions.

Linguistics means language. The dictionary defines it as the structure of language, divided into two subfields: phonetics—the study of speech sounds in their physical aspects; and phonology—the study of speech sounds in their cognitive aspects. In NLP we look at both of these aspects—what you say, and how you say it. But language is not restricted just to the spoken word. If neuro is the incoming signal, linguistics is how you interpret the content of the incoming signal. Your subconscious works in symbols. Linguistics converts your neuro data into symbols, for your subconscious to process. In this regard you convert from the following input:

- Pictures
- Sounds
- Feelings
- Tastes
- Smells
- Words (self-talk)
- Thoughts

Programming is the way we think, the way we process information, and the way we act. An analogy is operating software on a PC. We think, process and act in order to achieve a desired outcome. This "software" is a combination of:

- Genes (nature)
- Upbringing (nurture)
- Mood (happy/sad/joyful/depressed/etc.)
- Parents/family
- Modeling on key people
- Ethnicity
- Environment
- Experiences
- Feelings
- Intuition

So, we receive signals (neuro), interpret these signals into a language we understand (linguistics), and then run this language through our subconscious mind which is coded with motivating and demotivating drivers (programming):

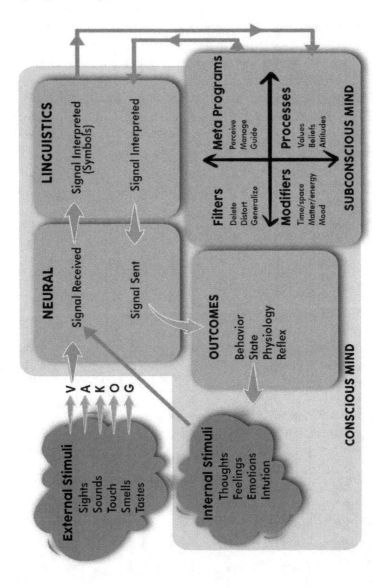

Consider this diagram. External stimuli such as sights, sounds, touch, smells and tastes are received by our five senses and sent to the brain for processing. They are joined by any internal stimuli we have created, such as thoughts, feelings, emotions, and intuition. The neural part of the mind sends the data to the linguistic part of the brain, which converts this data into symbolic data that the subconscious can understand. The subconscious, like a computer, applies a whole bunch of parameters (filters, values, beliefs, memories) to the symbolic data, and sends symbolic data back to the linguistic part of the brain. This is interpreted back into a language the neural part of the mind can understand. The neural mind then triggers an emotional or physical action.

We then assess the outcome of our action(s). If the desired outcome met our expectation, this reinforces that the model is working. If the desired outcome does not meet our expectation, it causes our subconscious program to be reprogrammed. The resulting experiences are the major event in modifying and updating our internal "software."

Our desired outcome is predicated on our concept of pain and pleasure. We perform an action to achieve pleasure, and this action is controlled and performed by our program (our mindset). The actual outcome is then processed by us, and we translate it into a perceived experience. Although it is a "perceived" experience, our perception is our reality. This is a "real" experience for us. This experience either met our pleasure expectation (and therefore reinforced our model and program), or it triggered pain signals (forcing changes). Two things happen as a result, often simultaneously: our value system might be modified by the experience, but our program will certainly be optimized (updated). Where our value system was changed, this will also modify our program:

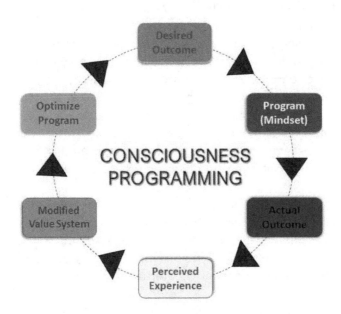

An interesting thing to note in this diagram is that our outcomes create internal stimuli which we process to create our outcomes. The majority of what we create (behavior, emotions, etc.) is self-generated. This is the whole premise of NLP—you are responsible for your current and future situation. You are not dependent on external factors.

Everything Tells a Story

It is not just our words that indicate our mindset. Our mindset is certainly displayed in what we say. But this verbal content is only 7% of what we are communicating; our tonality, the way we say things, represents 38%. Finally, our physiology (eye movement, facial expressions, etc.) accounts for a whopping 55% of what we are communicating!

At first this might seem unbelievable. But consider the various physiologies that can be displayed:

- Posture (e.g. slouching, or "in your face")
- Appearance (neat, untidy, formal, informal)
- Head movements (nodding, shaking)
- Expressions (laughing, crying, angry)
- Body space (too close? too far?)
- Body contact (tender touch? aggressive touch?)
- Eyes (open, squinting, angry, laughing, winking)
- Hand movements (hidden, waving, gesturing)
- Skin tone (normal, angry red, apoplectic purple)
- Word tone (loud, soft, angry)
- Etc.

We make prolific use of digital communication, and this leads to a lot of communication disconnect. Emoticons were introduced to bridge this gap in text, so that we could convey the tone of the message sent. I will often add an emoticon to a text to convey the correct tone.

Our Perception is Not the Only Reality

The world I see is different from the world you see. We might be seeing this world around us, but we all see it differently. As the input comes in, we apply filters. Our filters are how we treat the incoming signals. These filters are different in all of us as they have been shaped by our life's experiences—and as we have all had unique life experiences this cannot be identical. This is why two people might watch the same event and record something different. I remember as a kid arguing with a friend of mine: we disagreed about the color of a common tennis ball—for me it was yellow, and for him a lime green. Same tennis ball, different filters, different experience.

We create our "map of the world" based on our experiences, modeling, culture, beliefs, and filters. Yours is not wrong. But we need tolerance of other people's models – for them, their version is as real as yours.

Filters

Delete – we are inundated with information, possibly 10 million pieces of data per second. If we did not delete most of the data, we would be overwhelmed. For our self-preservation we need to delete information we no longer need, but are we possibly deleting useful data? Is it possible that our inner rules of deletion are incorrect?

Distort – we apply rules and filters to the incoming data. What are these rules? Are we applying them correctly?

Generalize – we chunk pieces of information into manageable units, and this is generalization. We have rules for this generalization—are they correct?

Time/space – we apply our understanding of time and space, which includes memories and timing of events.

Matter/energy – at the time of processing data, our mood, feelings and emotions play a big part. If we are low in energy, or tired, we might make "worse" decisions than if we were in a high energy phase.

Linguistics – this involves the hierarchy of ideas (levels of abstraction and specificity), the meta model (questions for uncovering cause and effect), linguistic presuppositions (natural assumptions in language) and the Milton Model (hypnotic language patterns).

Memories – the results of previous actions are stored and used as a scorecard. We know from experience what meets our desired outcome, and what doesn't.

Decisions – decisions at all levels affect our choices. Formal laws, preferences and inner desires are all decisions.

Meta programs – processing is affected by our perceptions, our need to manage the outcomes, need to guide the process, and history of experiences.

Beliefs – morals, culture, ethics, ethnicities, values and attitudes all play an important role in processing information.

It might be difficult to see the impact/effect of these filters. This table gives an idea, and we will all probably have used some of these in our lives:

Filter	Example
Positive Filtering	Taking only the positive details/aspects and deleting the negative ones.
Negative Filtering	Taking only the negative details/aspects and deleting the positive ones.
Polarized Thinking	Things are all black/white, good/bad, etc. If it is not perfect, we are a failure.
Negative Focus	We are consumed by a single negative (e.g. our ex-partner).
Over-generalization	Based on a single incident, we assume all similar incidents will go the same way.
Judging	Extreme form of generalization, describing an event with hyperbole to convince ourselves/others that our view is correct.
Maximizing	Magnifying or exaggerating facts to support our viewpoint.
Minimizing	Reducing or shrinking facts to undermine a viewpoint.
Mind Reading	We assume what people are going to say, and/or how people feel.
Jumping to Conclusions	We assume a negative (or positive) even though there is no evidence to support it.
Prediction	Acting out behavior commensurate with an outcome that has not happened.
Catastrophizing	Always expecting a disaster, we assume the worst and predict doom and gloom. What if? scenarios are always negative.
Personalization	Always assuming what is said is about us, because of us, or a reaction to us. We constantly compare ourselves to others.
External Control	We have no control, are "controlled" by others or our environment and see ourselves as a victim. (Victim)
Internal Control	We are responsible for everybody and/or everything. (Rescuer)

Filter	Example
Blaming	Others are responsible for our "bad" situation. Self-blame: we are responsible for our "bad" situation.
Righteousness	Our version of the truth is the only one. All others are wrong and/or inferior.
False Laws	All people should behave and act according to our model, culture, values, ethics.
Emotional Reasoning	What we feel is who we are. If we feel clumsy, this makes us clumsy.
Change Motivation	Our picture of achievement/success affects our behavior.
Global Labeling	One or two negative qualities are sufficient for a general negative for that aspect.
Life of "Job"	Everything seems to go wrong, and it's OK because we deserve it. We are not worthy. Or we accept it because there is a reward at the end.
Reward Fallacy	We feel bitter or marginalized when expected rewards do not materialize for hard work or sacrifices.

Modeling

From when we are born, we observe the world in action: we notice behavior we believe is effective, and what is not effective. Our model of the world and how it works is impacted, specifically, by the people around us, and especially by our primary caregiver (usually Mom), and secondary caregiver (usually Dad). The ethnic, cultural and environmental world around us also helps to shape who we are, what we believe, and how we think. We then model ourselves on this view of the world.

Our model consists of three elements:

1. Beliefs and value systems
2. Physiology
3. Strategies

Any part, or all of your modeling, can be changed – reprogrammed – by yourself.

Release Desire, Judgement and Discrimination

Re-evaluate your desires, and the value system driving those desires. Our desires are based on our picture of the world: how it should be, what I should have, how we compare, how others should behave. It is our continual desires that lead to pain, desperation, depression, frustration and a sense of failure. If we did not put so much value on achievement of our conscious desires, we would not encounter the massive emotional lows. When we constantly desire, we are in effect negating what we currently have. This is a sense of non-gratitude.

When we judge and/or discriminate, we are in essence judging ourselves; we are discriminating against ourselves. Consciousness is experiencing this world through your life. When you die, you will experience this world through another life - or even weirder – there is a possibility that you will experience the world through everybody's life. Think about that for a moment: if you were to experience everybody's life, how would you treat everybody else and how would you want to be treated?

A parallel argument is that you created your world and everything in it. If that is so, you are only judging yourself!

Forgiveness

Unforgiveness is now a recorded medical condition, and generally causes chronic anxiety. When we do not forgive, we carry around a toxic burden of anger, hatred, revenge and/or dislike. These negative emotions create a toxic cocktail of adrenalin and cortisol, which impact on our immune systems. Recent studies indicate that 61% of cancer patients have forgiveness issues.

> **Anger causes poisons to be secreted from the glands. No one can hate his neighbor and not have stomach or liver trouble. No one can be jealous and allow the anger of same and not have upset digestion or heart disorder.**
> **Edgar Cayce**

On a metaphysical level this fits in with the concept that we are all one. The anger/hatred/revenge/dislike is being heaped on ourselves, with obvious negative impacts.

Perspective

If we see the Moon near the horizon, we may notice that it appears huge. This isn't due to its distance, but rather an effect known as the "Moon Illusion," where our brain perceives the Moon to be closer when we see it on the horizon than when up above, thus overcompensating and tricking us into thinking it is bigger. We may look at a cloud and think we see a specific shape or pattern which does not exist – this is called "pareidolia". Our mind is full of "facts" that we believe, but they are not real.

The theory of relativity applies here, as it does for most of your life: we may have witnessed something happen, but it is from our perspective, influenced by our understanding of the world.

The human sympathetic system is quicker to respond than the parasympathetic, typically leading to an emotional overreaction, or action without reason. While we are on Earth we tend to take things very seriously. But we are forgetting the big picture—we will live sixty or seventy or eighty years and then pass on. Did our views really matter? Did our constant anger or depression help us? Was focusing more on making money and less on our family the right thing to do? One potential exercise here is to picture ourselves on our last day on Earth and consider: "What was important? What did I want to achieve? What personality did I wish to project? What do I want my legacy to be after I have gone? What lessons did I come to learn?"

The simple fact is none of us know where we came from, or where we are going to. But our compassion tells us that we are all made of the same stuff. Treat another as you would have them treat you. No one is superior or inferior to you.

You have created standards for yourself and other people and set stipulations in your mind. When these standards are not met, you get upset. Your attachment to pre-specified outcomes causes you to become angry, sad, depressed, anxious, jealous or hurt. Happiness is not the absence of problems. It is having the ability to deal with the challenges of life.

In your life, of ten things perhaps two are bad and eight are good. Why do you focus on the two bad things and not the eight good things? Perhaps transfer your focus to all the positives in your life. When we focus on the positive we lift our vibrational energy. When we lift our vibrational energy, positive things start to happen!

> **There is no good or bad, but for the thought that makes it so.**
> **Shakespeare**

Sense of Purpose

Another great quote from Viktor Frankl refers to sense of purpose: "A man who becomes conscious of the responsibility he bears toward a human being who affectionately waits for him, or to an unfinished work, will never be able to throw away his life. He knows the 'why' for his existence and will be able to bear almost any 'how'."

The Japanese have a word *Ikigai* meaning "a reason for being." Everyone, according to the Japanese, has an *Ikigai*. Finding it requires a deep and often lengthy search of self. Such a search is regarded as being very important, since it is believed that discovery of one's *Ikigai* brings satisfaction and meaning to life. The concept and process of *Ikigai* helps a person proceed towards self-realization.

Philosopher Daniel Dennett was right all along in asserting that the secret of happiness is to "find something more important than you are and dedicate your life to it." This is a sense of purpose.

Consider the following Ikigai diagram. Is your purpose a passion, a mission, a profession or a vocation?

Studies of people with cancer underline the fact that having a sense of purpose is a positive aspect of those who beat or controlled their cancer.

When we have a sense of purpose we focus less on the negative aspects of life. Elements such as stress and anxiety have less impact on us. We are less susceptible to depression-like diseases. We recover from colds and flu quicker than the average person. We are less likely to develop an addiction. There are so many examples of why having a sense of purpose is good for our health.

State of Flow

Mihály Csíkszentmihályi, an Italo-Hungarian psychologist, created the psychological concept of "flow." As you can see from the diagram below, a person with low skill level performing a task with low challenge level will be in a state of "apathy." The opposite would be a person with high skill performing a challenging task. This person is in a state of "flow."

In order for us to achieve happiness, we should all strive to be in the flow zone. With a sense of purpose one acquires the skills, over time, for that purpose. Our sense of purpose is naturally challenging, otherwise it would not be *Ikigai*.

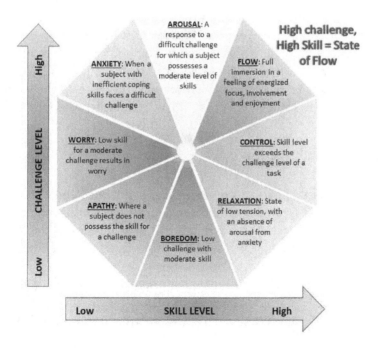

Optimism

Throughout this book there is a recurring theme of "what you think is what you become." Consider, then, an optimist versus a pessimist. An optimist will look on the bright side of a bad event, will have expectations of happiness and good fortune and will generally exude hope. A pessimist assumes something will go wrong—if it can go wrong it will—looks on the downside of any event and generally exudes doom and gloom. If what you think is what you become, then an optimist and a pessimist are self-fulfilling prophecy machines.

Optimists recover better from medical procedures, have healthier immune systems and live longer, both in general and when suffering from conditions such as cancer. Pessimists' constant negative outlook continually evokes the fight or flight response. In itself this leads to illness and stress, and thus the pessimist fulfils a self-fulfilling prophecy.

Optimism is more than just believing in a positive outcome. It encompasses stopping criticizing self and others, stopping judgment of self and others, and acceptance and forgiveness. Why accept and forgive? Because everything will work out. Bad things will continually happen to you—they are there for a reason. The reason is for you to learn a lesson, to improve your consciousness level. You might not be able to control events in your life, but you can control your response to the events. If your response is aligned with optimism, your life will be happier and less stressful. You decide.

Overcome Negative Thinking

Earlier I discussed how our primitive mind is primed to be alert for bad news as a result of an old self-preservation habit. We are naturally the seekers of bad news. How is it that some people have ditched this behavior, or diminished it so that it does not adversely affect them?

You become what you think, and therefore a mind diet of negative thoughts will lead to negative outcomes. Positive thoughts lead to positive outcomes; therefore it is in your interest to make the leap from negative to positive thinking. This is spelled out in the section on optimism earlier.

It takes practice to become aware of your thoughts, and it seems to be a bit of a consciousness exercise. It is very easy to just keep thinking thoughts and let them spew out uncontrolled. To change a thought requires awareness of the thought, and then application to change the thought from negative to positive. This takes some effort, but the rewards are worth it:

- ❖ State the intent to stop negative thoughts (say it out loud as well!)
- ❖ Start monitoring your thoughts
- ❖ Stop the negative thought and change it to a positive thought. You may think this is easier said than done, however there are always two sides to everything, look for the other side of the coin. Look for the good
- ❖ Stop criticizing self and others and events
- ❖ Stop judgments of self and others
- ❖ Stop complaining
- ❖ Practice acceptance

Remember that most things happen for a reason. In terms of consciousness growth, Steve Pavlina states the following:

"You can actually learn to embrace the negative thoughts running through your head and thereby transcend them. Allow them to be, but don't identify with them because those thoughts are not you. Begin to interact with them like an observer . . . It's been said that the mind is like a hyperactive monkey. The more you fight with the monkey, the more hyper it becomes. So instead just relax and observe the monkey until it wears itself out . . . Recognize also that this is the very reason you're here, living out your current life as a human being. Your reason for being here is to develop your consciousness. If you're mired in negativity, your job is to develop your consciousness to the point where you can learn to stay focused on what you want, to create positively instead of destructively . . . If you don't like what you're experiencing, that's because your skill at conscious creation remains underdeveloped. That's not a problem though because you're here to develop it. You're experiencing exactly what you're supposed to be experiencing so you can learn."

Nature has a powerful law, the Law of Cycles. This is evident in the weather patterns for instance, and even the stock exchange. Things go "well" for a while, and things then go "badly." Every now and again you may get a cold, every now and then you may feel emotionally low. Your life will never be a continual upward line on a graph. It is a series of ups and downs. Learn to appreciate the ups. Learn to accept the downs, or appreciate them, for without the downs the ups wouldn't seem so great. The appreciation will increase the frequency and duration of the ups. A lesson will keep returning until you have learnt the lesson—acceptance of the downs will reduce their frequency and duration. What you focus on is what you attract.

Chapter 13 – Revelations...by Tracy

Recently I was so low, and I had been for quite some time. Our family had been through many challenges. They seemed to hit us one after the next, knocking us down and totally removing the wind from our sails. Our daughter was an addict, and as a parent, everything you know about being positive and looking on the bright side flies out the window when you are unable to take away your child's pain or make things different or better for them. The helplessness eats you up inside and completely destroys you. Our other daughter was battling to find her direction. She went through an awful break-up where her fiancé ghosted her, and just when she thought life was getting better, found herself in an intimidating and difficult position at work. This stress left her feeling completely out of sorts and suffering from a few PTS type issues to work through.

We had moved countries. We were defrauded of a large sum of money in the EB5 visa program, had three family members pass, and traumatically lost a cute Yorkie and beloved cat to coyotes that literally hid at the bottom of our yard in wait for our pets to potty. We had another beloved pet unexpectedly fall ill and pass. Had three businesses that we put almost everything we had into, fail. We sold jewelry, properties and other assets to cover the loss and found jobs in order to pay the rent. For the first time in more than 20 years I was an employee and not the employer, rising at the crack of dawn to a screeching alarm clock, rushing to get to work on time and being told what to do and how to do it.

On weekends I wouldn't get out of bed. I told myself I needed the respite and that soon I'd be back to my old self, but that didn't happen. I'm not much of a talker or sharer, I keep my feelings to myself and therefore didn't really have an outlet. I felt disconnected from joy. I was numb. I felt like this world was an absolutely awful place and couldn't understand why everyone wants to live in it. I was totally overwhelmed and probably clinically depressed and could not dig my way out of the dark.

My husband, Steve felt the same way, as did both our daughters – life was just too hard! A constant up-hill battle that was more than we wanted to handle. When my eldest daughter reached out, sharing that she didn't want to be alive, and knowing my youngest has also felt this way, the first thought that came to mind was for us to create a suicide pact. My daughter asked for a family meeting and we realized that we had to do something differently and make a change.

Steve took control of the meeting and shared a few pearls of wisdom that reminded me of what I know but stopped practicing and the best way to learn something, or in this case re-learn it, is to help someone else learn it too. I found myself motivated to help my daughters overcome their problems by imparting the things I know. It was at this meeting that Steve asked me to read through The Law of Creation and give my critique. Something just clicked!

Within two days I was vibrating so much higher than I had been and felt joy again. I wanted to share The Law of Creation with everyone. I wanted everyone to have the tools to make themselves feel like I was feeling and still am. I felt like my old self again. I've always been a positive person, where nothing keeps me feeling down for long, so it was extra difficult for me being as low as I had been for so long. I read the book in a day or two, rewrote some sections, made suggestions, and had so much fun. I had a purpose again that I was passionate about. I felt grateful again. I was so grateful that my oldest daughter had spoken out and called a family meeting. So grateful that Steve reconnected to his power and reminded me of what I know, so grateful for the lessons my youngest daughter has helped me learn, so grateful for the job I have that gets me out of bed each day, so grateful for the people who press my buttons – showing me what issues I still need to address in myself, just so grateful!

It filled every cell in my body and I think this feeling felt so powerful because it was in such contrast to how I had been feeling for the past few years.

I questioned whether I was fooling myself, whether I was pretending to be this happy to try trick my brain into believing I was happy but then realized – it is that easy. It is that simple. Find something that makes you feel better and keep doing that – keep finding a thought or an experience that keeps lifting your spirit! How you feel is a direct indication of where you're vibrating. Choose to vibrate higher and then let go and trust that is what you will do while you focus on everything you are grateful for.

While writing, reading and rewriting this book I have come to realize some things. I believe I inherently know all this information. Everything rang true to me, and while it was very interesting and profound, I feel as if I already knew it. I think this is because it is inherent in all of us, but it is not our instinct, which is why we don't live our lives according to these Laws. We live our lives trying to protect ourselves. Protect ourselves from pain. Everything we do is for us to feel good, and not get hurt. Well, I can tell you that there is a way to not feel pain, to not hurt! When you are feeling pain, anger, hurt, sadness or any one of the other fear-based emotions we suffer from, know that you are out of alignment with love. Be excited that the emotion you are feeling is guiding you to feel better. Thank it and feel better.

You see, when you are vibrating with love and gratitude, it is impossible to feel anything other than good! There is always a different perspective than your current reality. Find a different perspective and your world changes. How you perceive everything is up to you. You can live any reality you want and living a loving grateful reality is all it takes to be permanently happy. It is impossible for pain and hurt to reside in the same space as love and gratitude at the same time. Impossible.

Don Miguel Ruiz in The Mastery of Love explains that "Mastering a relationship is all about YOU. The first step is to become aware, to know that everyone dreams his own dream." What Ruiz refers to here is the same as what books like The Disappearance of the Universe by Gary Renard and the script A Course in Miracles refer to – this reality is not real, we have created it by virtue of what we think and believe and is therefore likened to a dream, and each person's dream is unique to themselves. No one's dream can be exactly like our own. Ruiz further explains that once you know this you can then be completely responsible for your own half of the relationship, which is you. "If you know that you are only responsible for half of the relationship, you can easily control your half. It is not up to us to control the other half. If we respect [the other half] we know that our partner, or friend, or son, or mother, is completely responsible for his or her own half of the relationship. If we respect the other half, there is always going to be peace in that relationship. There is no war."

When you know the difference between fear and love, you are able to become love. When you live love, you become clear in your communication. You begin to communicate your dream in a loving manner and everything around you responds accordingly. You are complete love. Nothing to protect. Nothing to worry about. Nothing to stress about. Just pure love. You begin to see the beauty around you. The beauty in everything. If you don't see beauty (which is another form of love) in your enemy, then you are not vibrating with love. You see, if you are love, then you see the beauty in everything, because your love does not depend on the object of your love, your love is dependent on your state of being. So, whether the person or situation becomes different, or a friend turns to foe, does not matter, because your love is not dependent on anything around you, anything outside of you. Your love is a state of being. You simply love!

This book helped me connect with my real self. I FELT the gratitude and it affected my whole body. There is thinking about what you are grateful for and then there is knowing what you are grateful for. The difference is emotion. Think with enthused emotion and you begin to make a change.

You can create anything you desire. What will you create?